Watermark:

Vietnamese American
POETRY & PROSE

Edited by
Barbara Tran,
Monique T.D. Truong &
Luu Truong Khoi

ASIAN AMERICAN WRITERS' WORKSHOP • NEW YORK

WATERMARK:
Vietnamese American Poetry & Prose

© 1998 Barbara Tran, Monique T. D. Truong and Luu Truong Khoi

Library of Congress Number 97-78154

ISBN 1-889876-05-4   (cloth)

ISBN 1-889876-04-6   (paper)

Distributed by
TEMPLE UNIVERSITY PRESS
1-800-447-1656

Cover Art: ©1997 Thien Do

The text of this book is set in Sabon and Officina Serif.

Cover and Book Design: Thien Do, Monsoon Advertising, San Francisco, California.

Typesetting: Michelle Yung and Julie Ho

Published in the United States of America by The Asian American Writers' Workshop, New York.

Table of Contents

Watermark

from "Live by water, die for water"
Huynh Sanh Thong

[T]he word for "water" and the word for "a homeland, a country, a nation" are spelled the same way in the romanized script and are pronounced the same way: *nước*....

This is an instance where, by synecdoche, a part—the most essential part—has come to represent the whole: water, as the most precious resource of the homeland for growing crops (in particular, rice) has come to stand for the homeland itself. Those who have not discerned that dual acception of the one word *nước* have missed the origin of Vietnamese culture and what merges all its disparate elements into a coherent system....

Nước...remains the word with the most pervasive denotations and connotations in the Vietnamese vocabulary. It encompasses multifarious meanings, and it is resonant with subtle undertones capable of arousing the strongest emotions. In different contexts, it has to be translated by scores of different English words. It means still water, water that ebbs and flows or the tide, water that runs or rivers and streams. Water, needed for growing rice to eat, is also needed for drinking. *Nước* is the drinking water from a well or any beverage. It is the juice from fruits, too. Water is so appreciated as the basic thirst-quencher by the poor and the rich alike that daily meals are simply referred to as "rice and water" *(cơm nước)*. Indigents who own few utensils and lack such things as bowls and cups "(eat) rice from a small pot and (drink) water from a flask" *(cơm niêu nước lọ)*. The well-to-do can afford "white rice and clear water" *(cơm trắng nước trong)*. *Nước* is any liquid or some body fluid. It is the outward gloss, the "water" of a diamond, the complexion of a skin. It is the pace of a runner, the gait of a horse. It is the move on the chessboard or a way to play your cards. Broadly, it is a step you take in order to reach some goal. It is a pass you come to, and also a way out of the difficult spot. And more.

But the most significant derivation from the meaning of *nước* as "water" is the concept of people who have gathered near a body of water to grow rice for one another, and founding a stable community, sharing rain and drought, plenty and famine, peace and war: from "water," its basic meaning, *nước* has come to designate "the homeland, the country, the nation." It is in this ultimate acception that the monosyllable *nước* reverberates through the deepest and farthest recesses of the Vietnamese collective unconscious and stirs there the most potent feelings. The nation's fateful course, marked by ups and downs, is figuratively rendered as a "tide of water" *(vận nước)* with its ebb and flow. The highest virtue demanded of a Vietnamese is that he or she "love the *nước*" *(yêu nước)*. The worst opprobrium that can attach to any individual is that he or she has "sold out the *nước*" *(bán nước)*. To say in English that a man has "lost his country" is not the same as to say in Vietnamese that he has "lost the *nước*" *(mất nước)*. If the English phrase sounds almost abstract, the Vietnamese expression evokes an ordeal by thirst, the despair of a fish out of water....

The Brochure

Christian Langworthy

The movie is not worth the eight-fifty that I had paid, so while it is playing,
    I begin thinking of a vacation, a break from the daily grind.
The city is windy, and the sun lathers the buildings with a colloquial warmth
as people walk home from work in the latter stages of
                     the blank evening.
Excuse me, I ask. I am not from the city. Could you tell me where I am and
what it is I
am supposed to do? But no one responds as they hurriedly walk away.
I go down the long footstep of echoes.
        that is the city
until I am back in my room again, ready to inspect a copse
        of red carnations
and the picture of a young woman with lilacs in her hands
as she is kissing someone.
Who she is I will never know and on the table lies the travel brochure.
      Nevertheless, I walk into the garden where red, peach,
        and blue butterflies fight
against the pelting rain that has just started.
      So, we will not go to Coney Island, she says. Though it is a light rain
and the sun appears less threatening. We will not stroll on the boardwalk or watch
the amateur people divvying up the roles of our lives.
      But cotton candy is on my mind
for I have tasted the pink and blue sugar that has been spun through
the years of my tongue
stained with the same food coloring darkening the tongues of all the short
and tall children. We will not go to Coney Island, I say. We will not ride the Cyclone.
And she asks me to hold onto her
blue tongue and so I do, naming her "Lady With Blue Tongue."
We sleep together of course and sleep apart all covered up, and she bears me
many children who on Sundays
      stand along the stretch of river and smoke cigars
while peddling monkeys in little parkas. Oh, how she hates Mondays.

A vacation is in order for the tired ones, and we must as always travel to
exotic locales—
    Timbuktu or Buenos Aires, but we must know
where we are coming from for that is the beginning of the vacation.

This summer the mosquitoes understand the shadows
as if all the rooms are empty. The crowds jockey into position,
enamored of the city of
angels, but it is pleasant these days under the banyan tree when the marimba
            band plays, dabbling with greatness, wearing nothing but figs
and delighting the worn hearts being dragged by.
    She hands me back my twisted hand, saying,
Do you recall the misery of the mall and the red, hot chili peppers?
Is it possible that we can still be friends?
Even now, my attention span is short.
In her red, faded dress she looks so attractive
    that I dump all of my dim wares into the green river
winding its way through the green-breasted days of summer comforting
our city of angels.

A French couple in front of me talk about the movie
while it is still nearing its end. It is in Tuscany. There are fields of gold
and green, sloping hillsides. A girl is riding a bicycle down a narrow, winding road.
            She falls while making a turn.
A young lad happily carrying a bouncing dead rabbit
        killed by his steel trap
stops by the roadside to tend to her. He sets the rabbit
down on the red soil of the road.
He is thin and handsome with dark complexion, and he helps her to stand up.
She says that she is okay and thanks him. They look into each other's eyes and then
        she rides away.
    Oh, summer that I have never had!
How I want to be there! On that road of red soil, surrounded on both sides
by red, yellow and blue flowers. How the insects must sing in the cool
shadows of the road
            cutting through the green hillsides and fields of gold!

Up Over Boulder Hill

Dao Strom

My father is a big man. Once I watched him wrestle with our Newfoundland mutt Hobie on the kitchen floor. That was the time Hobie came back from his morning run with his snout full of porcupine quills, and they were all sticking out around his nose like a new set of whiskers. Dad held the dog around the chest with his left arm, holding his front paws down with his thick, brown forearm, and used his other hand to pull the quills out one by one with the pair of tweezers Mom used to use on us to pull splinters out of our fingers whenever we got them. Hobie is a large dog. When I was younger I used to ride on his back and pretend he was a horse.

Later, Dad had said, "It's a good thing that porcupine didn't have rabies." Just to be sure, though, Dad kept Hobie locked up in the utility room for a week afterwards so that we could watch and see if he started to act strangely. The only thing that happened was, Hobie barked a lot and scratched the plaster off the walls. If Hobie had got rabies, he would've had to be put to sleep or shot. I feel bad saying it, but I was a little disappointed, not because I wanted Hobie gone or anything, but because I was kind of curious to see what an animal with rabies acted like. I never said so to my dad, of course, because I never say much to my dad ever. My dad isn't a talkative kind of man.

Once I'd heard Jane Hopkins, who delivers the milk and whose father buys meat from my father, telling my older brother Adrian that she'd heard from her parents that my father once killed a man. The man he killed was the man my mother was really supposed to marry, that's how come my mom married my dad, because she was scared that he might kill her, too. Dad killed the man up on Boulder Hill, behind where the pigpen is now, where the big stump Dad and the other men use to chop firewood on is, and that's why my dad only lets us go up there if he's with us, is what Jane said, because he's afraid we might accidentally discover where he buried the body.

The next afternoon after I'd heard that, I asked Dad about it while he was smoking his pipe on the front porch. At first, he got mad and yelled at me that only a "stupid girl" would believe such a thing about her own father. I was younger then and started to cry. Dad put out his pipe, set it down on the porch railing, went over and picked me up, and said he would prove to me how silly I was being, and then he took me up to Boulder Hill and showed me how it was impossible for anything to be buried up there because the ground there was all rock.

I said, "But you could've done something else with it."

He laughed at me and said, "Katie, your Mommy and I got married because we fell in love, all right?"

I never really believed Jane's story, of course, but I have to admit it was always sort of in the back of my head whenever I looked at my dad. Later, when I told Adrian, he said he'd heard that Dad had chopped up the body and fed it to the pigs, which is something Adrian probably made up himself because that's how he was.

Back then, my mom was real pretty, and all the boys in town were in love with her and wanted to marry her, is what Mom'd told us before. She was so popular, even the captain of the football team was her boyfriend for awhile. Dad was just a boy from out of town who worked for a little while fixing cars for Mom's dad, and just happened to get lucky.

* * *

It was January right before Super Bowl Sunday the year I was twelve when Russell Nunn showed up looking for work. He was from out of state and on his way out West to maybe get married, he wasn't sure, he said, because he only knew the girl from writing letters to her. He was looking to work a week or two to get some more traveling cash. Dad didn't like him right off because, he said, he was aimless, and aimless boys are always up to no good. Dad hired him anyhow because he needed the extra help. There was the old trailer across the horse pasture for him to sleep in, three meals a day, and fifty dollars a week pay.

I saw Russell Nunn first before anyone else did when Dad sent me down the road to look for one of the turkeys that'd got out of the shed the night before and Dad had figured had probably drowned itself in the rain. The sun was shining when I climbed up the grassy bank that leveled out onto the road, though, and when I looked down the road I saw a man standing right out on the double yellow line. I knew right away that he wasn't from around here because I got a funny feeling in my stomach with my very first sight of him. It was a feeling I'd never got before, but somehow inside of me I knew it meant something big was going to happen, though I had no idea what exactly.

He was tall and dressed in layers of dark-colored clothing. He had a stick in his hand and was poking at something lying in the road, which I realized was our missing turkey. The man walked in a circle around the dead turkey. The light from the sun behind him made a shimmering outline of his body and made his legs look thin and wavy, and his hair blew back when he walked, and that was my first sighting of Russell Nunn. I watched him stop at the side of the road and bend down and reach for something in the grass, and then I slid back down the grassy bank. I never told anyone I'd seen him there, not even him. He turned up at our porch a half hour later with the dead turkey slung by its feet over his shoulder. He was carrying a dirty gray backpack and wearing faded black jeans and an old green-and-white football jersey with the number twenty-one on it, which was how old he was, he said. Twenty-one was also how old Dad was when he and Mom got married.

Right off, Dad put him to work shoveling dry dirt into the pigpen to firm up the mud. I sat on the pigpen fence and watched him. He'd taken off his jersey and hung it on a tree branch. Underneath, he had on a T-shirt with the sides slit open, and I could see his ribs whenever he stretched or bent. His eyes were large and blue, and his hair was dark brown streaked with dark blond. His skin was burnt red where his cheekbones stuck out. The only things he said to me were "What's your name?" and, after I'd told him it, "Katie's a nice name." He took a break to smoke a cigarette, and that's when my father came trudging towards us across the horse pasture carrying a potato sack over his shoulder.

He got himself and the bag through the barbed wire fence and reached the pigpen, where he nodded at Russell and said, "Come gimme a hand burying this poor bird, eh?"

Russell leaned back on the fence and took out his cigarettes. He shook one out of the pack and looked around, then put the cigarette between his lips and said, "Too much rock round here to be burying anything in, don't y'think?"

The sack slipped from Dad's grasp and landed on the ground with a thick-sounding thud. Dad looked hard at Russell and narrowed his eyes. "What do you suggest instead?"

Russell lit his cigarette. The metal lid of his lighter opened and closed with a sharp snapping sound. "Seems like you don't waste nothin' when you feed them pigs," he said.

Dad's jaw moved slightly, and he looked mean all of a sudden. "My pigs don't eat meat."

Russell hooked his arm across his midsection and looked over his shoulder like he wasn't really paying attention to Dad. "They get bigger if they do, don't they?"

"I don't know where you're from, mister," said Dad, "but that is not how I do things around here."

Russell looked down at the cigarette shrinking away in his fingers. He was as tall as Dad, I noticed, but Dad was much broader. After a second, Russell said, "Why don't I go chop some firewood b'fore the rain comes again, eh?"

Dad said that would be a good idea in a tone that made it sound like he didn't think it would be a good idea at all, and then he took me with him back to the house, leaving the potato sack there by the pigpen with Russell. Before dinner, Dad was in the kitchen complaining to Mom that the problem with hired help was, "You never had no idea where they'd come from or been," he said. He seemed angrier about Russell than he ever had about anyone else, and that only made me more curious about Russell, I think.

That night, I watched out my bedroom window for the light to go out in the trailer across the horse pasture where Russell was staying, but it never did. Before I fell asleep, I saw Russell come out and sit on a stump with a shoebox full of letters in his lap. He sat cross-legged with one hand clenched in a fist around a clump of hair on top of his head. The light was still on when I looked out my window in the morning.

In the morning, Dad sent Russell round to the far side of Boulder Hill to dig holes for fence posts, and I went to school. The sun was shining through the bus windows on the ride there, and I noticed everyone's faces glowed orange. We baked peanut butter cookies during P.E. because it was an extracurricular-activity day. When I got home, I snuck out to Russell's trailer and left six cookies in a brown lunch bag on the doorstep.

The next day, I sat in a tree for three hours straight and watched him plant fence posts in the holes he'd dug. He was sweating even though the weather was damp and gray.

Al Deakins, who borrows Dad's chainsaw on a regular basis and helps Dad every year with packing and shipping the pigs after they're slaughtered, came by that afternoon to show off his new pit bull. It was a small, white, bow-legged dog named Shirley. Adrian wanted to know who Al thought would win in a fight, Shirley or our dog Hobie.

"Thing 'bout these kind of dogs," said Al, "they may be small but they're strong as hell where it counts. They've got a special nerve that when it's triggered and they attach their jaws t'somethin', they don't let go 'til there's nothin' left to hold on to."

"I never liked them kind of dogs," Dad said.

"A man's gotta rely on someone," said Al back.

Russell passed by with an armload of firewood to put on the porch, and the pit bull began to bark. Al picked it up and put it in the cab of his truck, and then he and Dad went into the kitchen to look for something to drink.

I found Russell stretched out on a rock on the other side of Boulder Hill. He was on his stomach, writing on a tablet of paper. I sat down a few feet away with my chin on my knees.

"That a letter to that girl you're gonna marry?" I asked after a while.

He looked up like I'd startled him. "Girl?"

"You got a whole boxful of letters from her, don't you?"

"There's no girl I'm gonna marry," he said, and sat up. He tore off the sheets he'd written on and put them in his pocket, and I watched him. "Don't you got somethin' better t'do than watch me all the time?"

"No," I said, and asked, "Who're you writing to then?"

"No one. Just writing. Maybe I'd like there t'be a girl I write to, 'cept I don't know where she'd be. Maybe I'm traveling around looking for her, maybe I'm not." He lit a cigarette and pulled his knees into his chest. "I hate to be rude, Katie, but truth is I was writing so I wouldn't hafta talk out loud to anyone 'bout what I was thinking."

I wanted to ask what was he thinking then, but I couldn't get myself to, so I just sat and stared at him smoking his cigarette. He had his back turned slightly toward me, and I could see his shoulder blades showing through his old football jersey. I thought how much older he was than me and how many more things he'd done, and it occurred to me then how silly it was for me to even hope he could be friends with me.

When I got up to leave, he twisted around and looked at me with what I thought was a funny look, and he asked where I was going. I said maybe I was gonna go watch my dad feed the turkeys. He said, "Hold this for a sec," and handed me the lit cigarette from his mouth. I had to take a few steps forward to reach it, and for some reason that made me nervous. I stood there holding his cigarette, and what he did was, he pulled his jersey off over his head, and then he took back his cigarette and gave the jersey to me, and said I could wear it if I wanted to. He'd been captain of the varsity football team his last year in high school, is what he said, sticking his cigarette back between his lips and talking out of the corner of his mouth.

I took the football jersey from him, and later I noticed that there looked like there were bloodstains on one sleeve. When I asked about them, Russell said he'd got a bloody nose once when someone'd pushed him into a wall in a bar in New York City.

That night, I climbed out my bedroom window and down the porch and went and knocked on Russell's trailer door because I couldn't sleep. He'd been up looking at old sports magazines. He dug out an old football, and we went up onto the road, and he taught me how to throw and catch the ball very quietly. He said I caught on fast for a girl.

He ran ahead down the empty road, throwing the football out and running forward to catch it himself again. When I finally caught up to him, he was lying on his back spread out in the middle of the road with a smile on his face and staring up at the sky. I asked what was he doing, and he said for me to lie down on my back like he was. When I did, he said, "Have you ever seen so many stars?" I thought he was the most peculiar person I'd ever met.

He told me on the second night we walked down the road that the best part of his life so far was the time he'd lived on an island out in the middle of the Pacific Ocean itself. I'd never even heard of anyone who even knew someone who'd lived on an island. I had a picture in my head of an island as a beige-colored mound of sand with a palm tree on one side of it, sitting out in the middle of this huge, flat blue plane of water and a shark fin making a white trail in the water. Truth is, I'd never seen an island or the ocean even, for that matter. Russell, though, he said the weather was always warm and sunny there on that island, and he used to go jump off a cliff into the water first thing every morning, and then he'd eat breakfast sitting on a rock, drying off in the sun. He said he'd been really young then, so he couldn't remember exactly how he'd gotten onto the island, and he couldn't really remember how he'd left it, either. He'd just woke up one day and found himself whacking weeds in someone's yard and that's about how it'd been ever since, is how he said things had gone.

I liked to watch his face when he talked because I had to look up at him, and when I did I always saw the night sky huge and open behind him and the tips of his hair glowing blue and his eyes wet-looking because of the glow. Sometimes, looking at him would make me think strange thoughts, like I would pretend in my head that I could go back in time and meet Russell Nunn on his island, and I would know who he was and that we'd meet in the future, but he would have no idea who I was, except that I was a girl who could tell things about him that he hadn't ever told me.

* * *

I wore Russell's football jersey around the house for the next two days before Dad finally said anything. I know he noticed, though, because he'd look at me twice every time he saw me and then he'd look away. The jersey was too big and the sleeves hung down past my elbows. At dinner on the second night, Dad sat staring straight ahead, chewing, and not blinking, his butter knife sticking point up out of his fist, both fists on the table. He swallowed and said, "Katie, go take off that ridiculous shirt now." His knuckles were white, and his eyes were wide open and dry.

I changed, but I hung the football jersey up on a hanger in front of my window, just so I could look at it, but also so that anyone who happened to visit our house would see it. On Super Bowl Sunday every year, all the neighbors come over to our house for a barbecue and to watch the game, and I knew that this would be happening soon for this year. Dad saw and told me to take it down, so I did, but I put it up again once he'd gone to bed. I lay under the covers with the moon coming in my open window and Russell's football jersey flapping softly in the breeze.

That night on our walk, Russell and I got charged at by a barking dog. I jumped up into a tree, and the dog got Russell around the leg. He picked up a rock and started beating the dog on top of its head to get it to let go, but it wouldn't, so he kicked it real hard with his free leg, and it went flying sideways but was still hanging on. I could hear the dog grunting and the sound of Russell and the dog's feet, but otherwise Russell wasn't making any other noise. Russell reached for a bigger rock and slammed it into the dog's snout. The dog let go for one second, and Russell got loose and then went on slamming the dog in the face with the rock so that it couldn't get a chance to grab hold of him again. Russell had blood on his hands and running down his leg, too. He came and stood under the tree and asked me if I was going to come down.

"That's the Deakins' dog," I said.

"I'm losing blood here, Katie, you gonna come down or not?"

"You gotta do something with it, you can't just leave it there."

I watched Russell pick up the dog and carry it away somewhere. I didn't get down from the tree until he'd come back. His hands were clean, I noticed.

We went back to the trailer after that, and I watched while Russell cleaned up his leg where the dog'd bit him. The bite kept bleeding, and he got blood all over his pants and on two shirts cleaning himself up. I only had a few scrapes on my elbows from the tree bark.

"Why didn't you come down and give me a hand, huh, Katie?" he asked, tying up his bandage.

"I woulda got bit," I answered.

He winced as he picked his leg up and put it out straight on his bed. "Yeah, I guess you woulda."

I was sitting on the corner of the bed, flipping through one of his old sports magazines. "You're strange," I said.

"Why's that, Katie?" When I glanced toward him, he was looking at me in a weird way.

"You just are," I said.

"No, I'm not, you're just nervous." He sat forward, and I could see how large and round his pupils were, his eyes were staring so steady into mine. I couldn't talk, so I just stared back at him. Then, he blinked and reached for a cigarette and dangled it on his lower lip. "If there's a strange one between us, Katie, you're the one." He lit his cigarette and breathed out smoke. "I swear I've never known any twelve year-old, boy or girl, t'be as quiet and calm as you are." He dropped his ashes into a dirty coffee cup on the counter that was connected to the bed. He looked like he was concentrating on something. "Not sayin' that I often spend a lot of time with twelve year-olds. You're an exception, you should know that, Katie." He scooted forward and swung his legs over the side of the bed so that he was sitting next to me, keeping his hurt leg out straight. "I got a question I know I shouldn't ask, do you want me to ask it?"

"What is it?" When I looked sideways, I saw Russell's face looming so close that all I saw was a huge, tan blur and two rows of glowing white squares that were his teeth.

He looked down at his feet suddenly, and I saw his cheeks hollow all the way out as he sucked on his cigarette. "Aw, forget it," he said, and let out a little laugh. "I was just curious—I was just wondering if you'd ever kissed a guy b'fore or not. I'd at least kissed a girl a few times by the time I was twelve, I'm pretty sure."

"What'd you wanna know that for?" I said. I could feel a feeling like my stomach rising inside of me going on.

"Like I said, I was just curious," said Russell, and stood up and leaned against the trailer door.

"When was the last time you kissed a girl?"

"There aren't many girls I'd kiss. I hold kissing in an especially high regard." He extinguished his cigarette and lit another one and lowered himself carefully down on the bed.

I fell asleep in Russell's trailer that night. I woke up and the sun was rising. Russell had fallen asleep sitting up, and his hand was draped on top of my knee and part of my thigh, too. I looked at it and was amazed by how small my leg looked beneath it. I pulled away and suddenly noticed how cold the trailer was.

When I got back to my room, I saw that the football jersey was gone, and Dad was down the hill in back of the house, warming his hands over a small brush fire he'd started in the burn circle where we usually burn trash. I watched out the bathroom windows as he fed the fire with the remaining branches from trees that'd been chopped for firewood.

At breakfast, Dad didn't speak to anyone. Al Deakins came knocking on our door, and Dad went out on the porch, and the two of them talked standing close together in the corner for a long while. Jane Hopkins delivered the milk and said how she'd heard the Deakins had found their pit bull drowned in their swimming pool that morning, and they didn't know if the dog'd jumped in itself and knocked itself unconscious or if someone'd gone and thrown it in for some reason. Jane said Al Deakins was going around the neighborhood asking everyone if they'd seen or heard anything unusual in the night. Adrian said maybe the dog'd had rabies and drowned itself to death trying to drink too much because thirst was a symptom of rabies.

I was worrying about the whole thing and trying to act like I didn't know anything about it. I didn't know what else to do, so I took a walk down the road. I was sitting in the grass on the side of the road when Dad drove out in his truck and passed Roger Twomy, who was the local vet, going the opposite way. They sat with their engines idling a few feet down from me and talked to each other out their windows. Maybe I just imagined it because it was on my mind, but it sounded like my dad said, "I got myself a rabid man living in my horse pasture, Roger," and Roger answered back, "That's Nature tellin' you beware, Henry."

Al Deakins came by in the afternoon with his dead pit bull in the back of his truck and he hauled it out and dumped it in the dirt at the bottom of the porch steps and said he was leaving it there until someone came out and owned up to what really happened. It was wet and pinkish-colored and bloated, and there was a gash down the middle of its face. Dad was still out running errands. Adrian was the only one who came out onto the porch, and he only came out because he wanted to see a dead body. When Dad got home, Al said to him, "I hold you responsible for this, Henry." Dad walked in a circle around the dead dog with his hands in his pockets. He prodded the body with his foot, then stood there looking down at it for a long time as if no one else was around. Al said, "Did y'hear me, Henry? I'm holding you responsible for this. I think you know why."

"I'll take care of it," said Dad.

"I know you weren't involved directly, but I can't help but take it personally, I'm sorry, Henry," said Al as he was leaving.

Dad put the dead pit bull in a wheelbarrow and went out to the far side of Boulder Hill to bury it. Then, he went and knocked on the trailer door, and he and Russell were inside together for at least twenty minutes. Dad came back into the house with his jaw muscles tense and his face a little red. Before dinner, he walked through the living room with an armful of firewood while I was watching TV on the couch, and he said more out loud than to me directly that Russell Nunn was going to be gone in the morning, and that he didn't want me leaving the house, unless it was with himself, until then. I just said OK and looked at him once.

* * *

That evening, some boys on dirt bikes came down our driveway saying how they'd seen a deer stuck in a fence down the road. It was a young deer that'd tried to jump over the fence but didn't make it all the way and had got its leg twisted up in the crosswires somehow. Dad and Russell went down to see what they could do, and Adrian and I went, too. The fur on the deer's leg was rubbed away down to its skin, and you could see its flesh all raw and pink from it trying to yank its leg free. Dad said not to touch it because if it got the smell of humans on it, other deer wouldn't go near it again. Dad said it would get itself loose eventually and that if it didn't, well, that was just nature then. Russell went and got a pair of wirecutters even though, and he cut the deer loose. Adrian and I stood on the other side of the road, watching. It took a long time, and after a while, I turned around because I didn't want to watch anymore. Adrian kept poking at me and telling me to "look now" because the deer's leg was hanging off by its bone, until Dad heard him and told him to stop. I left and walked back up the road home by myself. I didn't feel so good after all that.

Later, while we were brushing our teeth before bed, Adrian told me how before Russell could cut the deer all the way loose, it had yanked away, and its leg had gone flying up into the air, and the deer had run away on three legs. Supposedly, the rest of the deer's leg was still lying in the field somewhere.

That night, I watched Russell hose the blood off of the wirecutters at the faucet by the side of the porch. I watched looking down from my bedroom window. Russell was barefoot with his sleeves and pant legs pushed up, and his skin glistened where it was wet from the water splashing onto it. I couldn't see his face, only the top of his head, and his hair looked soft and blue and shiny in the moonlight. I watched him rinse off his forearms and feet and dry them off on the old towel draped over the porch railing. Then, he stepped back into his boots and headed off across the pasture toward the trailer, swinging the wirecutters and looking up at the sky as he walked, and that was the last sighting of Russell Nunn I ever saw, and I'd knew it would be as I was watching him.

* * *

Something woke me up at dawn about the point where I could just begin to see the dim outline of the objects in my room. I got out of bed and went to the window. The sky was still dark but verging on dark turquoise, and there was a thin strip of orange and purple along the edges of the faraway hills, like the hint of a smile spreading across the countryside.

The air was chilly against my face as I leaned out the window. The silence was so big it made my ears feel like they were just wide open holes on either side of my head. I knew that somewhere off in the distance, eventually a rooster would crow and its crow would echo against the huge sky, and then little sounds like creaks and twirps and light switches and faucets running would start. But right then, it was silent. I thought how this was probably the only time when every creature was asleep because it was the time before the day animals and people had woke up and right after the night animals had gone to bed. It was the kind of silence like I imagined my elementary school teachers had meant when they explained how it was way up in space, past the moon and planets, farther up than I could even imagine. As I was listening to my own breathing, I felt a cool, airy feeling growing in my chest, expanding into my throat, too, and making the inside of my mouth seem bigger and colder than ever. Then, from below, I heard a noise like a bucket being kicked over.

I saw my father coming out of the trailer wearing his galoshes and gloves. He paused by the stump outside, and wiped his forearm across his face, and then closed the trailer door quietly behind him. He disappeared for a moment behind the trailer. Next I saw, he was pushing a wheelbarrow and it had two brown canvas potato sacks in it. He pushed the wheelbarrow across the horse pasture, through the gate on the far side, past the pigs, up over Boulder Hill and down the other side, where he disappeared out of view again. A rooster crowed in a neighbor's yard somewhere, and then I heard two loud noises, like cracks when a tree falls, so sharp-sounding they made the color of the sky just above Boulder Hill shift, for my eyes at least. Then, my father appeared at the top of the hill, walking with his shoulders so square and big they swallowed up his neck and made his head look like a small black egg stuck on top of a square black block, and the sun was lifting up behind him, making him glow around the edges. He came back down the hill, his galoshes crunching on the rocks of Boulder Hill. He had his ax over one shoulder and a tin pail swinging at the end of his other arm. I watched as he leaned over the pigpen fence and whistled to the pigs and then dumped the contents of the pail into the muddy feed trough.

Letter to My Bed

Linh Dinh

Disheveled bed, sentimental sponge, love of my life,
Witness to all my horrors, my Valdez spills, my crimes,
Black-faced farces, commedia dell'arte—*par-deux* and solo,
Hopped-up rants, weepy pleas, morning conversations,
Do not spill our confidential beans to enemy intelligence.
They have surrounded us on all sides tonight, bed,
And tomorrow night, and the night after tomorrow night.
You are the leaky boat on the South China Sea fleeing
Ho Chi Minh City; you are the wide gurney of my nightly dearth.

History

Thuong Vuong-Riddick

From China, the Yuen people traveled south, and killed
the Thai, the Khmers, the Mongs and the Chams from the
Kingdom of Funan. As a result of their "Marching towards
the South," the Yuen became independent, the Viet.

Then for ten centuries the Chinese waged war and killed
the Vietnamese and called Vietnam, Annam, which means
"The Pacified South."

The French killed the Vietnamese and
occupied the country for a century.
The Vietnamese who fought the French
were called Vietminh.
The French and the Vietnamese killed
the Vietminh (secretly helped by the Americans).
The Japanese killed the French.
The Japanese allied with the French killed
the Chinese and the Vietminh.
The Japanese helped the Vietnamese to proclaim
the Independence of Vietnam.
The Japanese killed the French and were defeated.
The Americans helped the Vietminh to become
    the Democratic Republic of Vietnam.

The French and their allies, the British,
killed the Vietminh.
The French, equipped by the Americans, lost to
the Vietminh, equipped by the Chinese.
The Americans took the place of the French.
The Vietminh were called the Vietcong.

The Vietcong, armed by China and the U.S.S.R.,
killed the Vietnamese and the Americans.
The Vietcong prevailed.

People fled overseas.

Seeds

Monique T.D. Truong

Two American ladies wish to retain a cook—27 rue de Fleurus. See caretaker's office, first floor.

"Yes, yes, they are still looking for a cook. You'll have to come back in an hour or two when they have returned from their drive. Just knock on those large doors to your left. They lead to the studio. What did you say your name was?

"Binh. Binh Nguyen."

"Beene? Beene, yes, that's easy enough on the tongue. You seem like a nice boy. Let me give you, let's say, a bit of advice—don't blink an eye."

"What?"

"Don't blink an eye. Do you understand?"

"No."

"Well, let's say, the two Americans are a bit unusual. Well, you'll see that for yourself as soon as the doors to the studio are opened."

"Did you say 'studio?' Painters?"

"No, no, a writer and, ummm, a companion. But that's not the point! They are très gentilles, très gentilles."

"And?"

"Well, no point, really. Except. Except, you should call her by her full name, Madame GertrudeStein. Always, Madame GertrudeStein. Just think of it as one word."

"Is that it? What about the other one?"

"Oh, yes, certainly, her name is Alice Toklas. She prefers Madame Alice."

"And?"

"Well, that's it. That's it."

"I'll be back in an hour then. Good-bye, Monsieur."

* * *

Two American ladies wish—

Sounds more like a proclamation than a help-wanted ad.

Well, of course, two American ladies in Paris these days would only "wish" because to wish is to receive; to want, well, to want is just not American. I congratulated myself on this rather apt and piquant piece of social commentary. Now if only I knew how to say "apt" and "piquant" in French, I could stop congratulating myself and strike up a conversation with the "petit garçon" sitting three park benches over. Ah, the irony of acquiring a foreign tongue is that you amass just enough cheap, serviceable words to fuel your desires and never, never enough lavish, imprudent ones to feed them.

It is true that there are some French words I have picked up quickly, in fact, words I can't remember never knowing. Like I had been born with them in my mouth, like they were the seeds and pits of a sour fruit that someone else ate and stuffed ungraciously into my own.

"Ungraciously? Ungraciously? *Troi oi,* I'll tell you who is ungracious. It's you, you ungracious, disrespectful, disappearing lout of a son. I taught you how to say 's'il vous plait,' 'merci,' 'Monsieur,' 'Madame,' so that you could work in the Governor-General's house. Your oldest brother, he started out like you. At the age of ten, he was just the boy who picked up after Madame's 'petit chouchou' after it did its business in every corner of the house, warping the wood floors with its shit and urine. Now, he's thirty and a sous-chef! Wears a crisp white apron and knows more French words than the local school teacher. He says that soon he's going to be promoted to...."

I have discovered only one true and constant thing in my life. It is that my father's anger has no respect for geography. Mountains, rivers, oceans, and seas, these things that would have otherwise kept an average man locked onto the hectare of land which he was raised from birth to call home; these things have never kept my father from honing in on me, pinpointing my location, and making me pay my respects. While his body lies deep in the ground of Saigon, his anger sojourns with his no-good son on a Parisian park bench.

Even here, he's found me.

"Unemployed and alone," he surmises, distilling my life into two sad, stinging words.

I try to protect myself with a knowing smirk. "Oh, you again? I thought I was dead to you, old man? 'No son of mine leaves a good job at the Governor-General's to be a cook! A cook on some leaky boat for sailors who don't even know how to say "please" or "thank you" in their own language not to mention in French. Old whores become *cooks* on boats, not any son of mine,' you said."

Sometimes, I cannot give enough thanks to your Catholic god, that you, my dear and violent father, are now merely cobbled together from my unwavering sense of guilt and my telescopic memories of brutalities lived long ago. Because a retort like that, a challenge like that, would have extracted from you nothing less than a slap in the face and a punch in the stomach. But now, my dear and violent father, who art up in heaven, you *will* dissipate in the face of my calm, cool smirk.

"Unemployed and Alone," however, obstinately refuse to retreat and demand that I address their needs before September disappears into October.

* * *

Two American ladies wish to retain a cook—

Hmmm...Americans. Hope their French is not as wretched as mine. What a fine household we would make, hand movements and crude drawings to supplement our mutual use of a secondhand language.

Though, contrary to what my father would tell you, the vocabulary of servitude is not built upon your knowledge of foreign words but rather on your ability to swallow them. Not your own, of course, but your Monsieur and Madame's.

The first thing I learned at the Governor-General's house was that when Monsieur and Madame were consumed by their lunatic displeasure at how the floors had been waxed, how the silver had been polished, or how the "poulet" had been stewed, they would berate the household staff, all fifteen of us, in French. But not the patois of dumbed-down French coupled with atonal attempts at Vietnamese that they'd normally used with us. No, this was a pure variety reserved for dignitaries and obtuse Indochinois servants. It's as if Monsieur and Madame were wholly incapable of expressing their finely wrought rage in any other language but their own.

Of course, we would all bow our heads and act repentant, just like the

Catholic priest had taught us. Of course, we would all stand there blissful in our ignorance of the nuances, wordplays and double entendres of that language which was seeking desperately to assault us. Oh, naturally, some words would slip through, but for the most part we were all rather skilled in the refusal and rejection of all but the most necessary.

Minh-The-Sous-Chef, as my father had renamed him, was always telling us how the French never tired of debating why the Indochinois of a certain class are never able to master the difficulties, the subtleties, the winged eloquence of the French language. I now suspect that this is a topic of discussion for the ruling class everywhere. So enamored with their differences, language and otherwise, that they have lost the instinctual ability to detect the defiance of those who serve them.

Minh-The-Sous-Chef used to be just Anh Minh, my oldest brother and the only brother who today can make me think of home. No one would have enjoyed this park bench and the shade of these forlorn chestnut trees more than he would have. Anh Minh believed absolutely and passionately that the French language would save us, would welcome us into the fold, would reward us with kisses on both cheeks. His was not an abstract belief. No, it was grounded in the kitchen of the Governor-General's house. He insisted that after Monsieur and Madame tasted his Omelette à la Bourbonnaise, his Coupe Ambassadrice, his Crème Marquise they would have no need to send for a French chef de cuisine to replace old Claude Chaboux. My father, like a soothsayer, declared that soon there would be the first Vietnamese chef de cuisine in the Governor-General's house.

So while the rest of us stood there dumbly experiencing the balletic surges of Monsieur and Madame's tirade, Anh Minh, alone, stood in agony. Lashed and betrayed by all those words he had adopted and kept close to his heart. Wounded.

Minh-The-Wounded, I began calling him in my prayers.

Old Chaboux died and a young Jean Blériot arrived from France to don the coveted title. Now, only an act of god, a bout of malaria, or a lustful look at Madame would hasten the departure of Chef Blériot, as he insisted on being called.

May 11, 1922, began the reign of Chef Blériot. Anh Minh stayed on in the kitchen of the Governor-General's to serve under yet another French chef, to cover for him once he begins to reek of rum, to clean after him once he can no longer see where the rim of the pot begins, sending handfuls of shallot and dashes of oil to season the tile floor. And me, what was I supposed to do? Twenty years old and still just a "garde-manger" sculpting potatoes into perfect little spheres, carving chunks of turnips into swans with the arc of their necks as delicate as Blériot's fingers, fingers that I instinctively wanted to taste. Equipped with skills and desires that no man would admit to having, what was I supposed to do?

* * *

Two American ladies wish to retain a cook—27 rue de Fleurus.

Prosperous enough area of town and two American ladies must have enough to pay a nice wage.

One of my skills, really it's more like a sleight of hand, that I've secured since coming to this city is an acumen for its streets. I know where they reside, where they dissolve discreetly into one another, where they inexplicably choose to rear their unmarked heads. A skill born from the lack of other skills, really. When each day is mapped for you by a wanton display of street names, congesting the pages of the help-wanted's; when you are accompanied by the stench of unemployability, well, you too will be forced into an avid, adoring courtship with the streets of this city.

Oh, I must admit that in truly desperate times, my intimate knowledge of the city has saved me. A mistress with a heart.

"Name any street. Go ahead, any street. I'll tell you where it is, Left Bank or Right Bank, exact locale even. Rue de Fleurus? It's that little street off the boulevard Raspail, near the Luxembourg Gardens."

I've earned at least several dozen glasses of marc that way. Frenchmen, Drunkmen love a challenge. The listeners, if any, often will ask me to repeat myself. Seems that my accented French is even hard on the ears of laborers. Once it's clear that I am there for their amusement, well, the rest is a transcendent performance. Fortunately, for me, I have no idea how to say "transcendent performance" in French because otherwise I would be compelled to brag and ruin the surprise. And they are always surprised. And they always try again. They'll name the street where their great-aunt Sylvie lived, where their butcher is located, where they last got lost; and then, when truly desperate, they'll name a street on one of the islands that cleave this city. By then, I am gone because too often their surprise deviates into anger.

"How can this little Indochinois, who can't even speak proper French, who can't even say more than a simple sentence, who can't even understand enough to get angry over the jokes that we are making at his expense; how can this Indochinois know this city better than me?"

It's like I promised them a bag of rotten apples and then they opened it and found, well, *me*. "Come see the little Indochinois who knows this city better than any Parisian!" All I need is a little monkey dressed in a suit better than my own, and I could join the ranks of the circus freaks, half-man-half-woman sword swallowers, and now "Binh-The-Human-Map-of-Desperation!"

But, these are hardly skills to impress any potential Monsieur and Madame with.

I have been in this city now for over three years. I have interviewed with and even worked for an embarrassing number of households. In my experience, they break down into two categories. No, in fact, there are three. The first are those who after a cat-like glimpse at my face will issue an immediate rejection, usually non-verbal. A door slam is an uncommonly effective form of communication. No discussion, no references required, no "Will you want Sundays off?" Those, while immediately unpleasant, I prefer.

Type-twos are those who may or may not end up hiring you but who will nonetheless insist on stripping you with questions, like an indelicate physical examination. Type-twos often behave as if they've been deputized by the French government to ferret out and to document exactly how it is that I have come to inhabit these hallow shores.

"In Paris. Three years."

"Where were you before?"

"Marseilles."

"Where were you before that?"

"Boat to Marseilles."

"Boat? Yes, well, obviously. Where did that boat sail from?"

"Alexandria."

"Alexandria?"

"Yes, Egypt."

And so like a courtesan, forced to perform the dance of the seven veils, I grudgingly reveal the names, one by one, of the cities that have imperceptibly carved their names into me, leaving behind the scar tissue that form the bulk of who I am.

"Hmmm...you say you've been in Paris for three years? Now, let's see, if you left Indochine when you were twenty, that would make you...."

"Twenty-seven, Madame."

"Four years unaccounted for!" You could almost hear them thinking.

Most Parisians can ignore and even forgive you for not having the refinement to be born amidst the ringing bells of their cathedrals, especially if you were born instead amidst the ringing bells of the replicas of their cathedrals, erected in far off colonies to remind them of the majesty, the piety of home. This is all to say that as long as Monsieur and Madame can account for your whereabouts in their city or in one of their colonies, well, then they can trust that the Republique and the Catholic Church have had their watchful eyes on you.

But now that I have exposed myself as a subject who has strayed, lived a life unchecked, ungoverned, undocumented, and unrepentant, I am again suspect. Before, I was no more of a threat than a cloistered nun. Now, Madame glares at me to see if she can detect the deviant sexual practices that I have surely picked up and am now, without a doubt, proliferating under the very noses of the city's Notre Dames. Madame now worries whether she can trust me with her little girls.

"Ah, Madame. You have nothing to worry about. I have no interest in your little girls. Your boys...well, that is their choice." She should hear me thinking.

The odds are stacked against me with this second type. I know. But I find myself again and again shamefully submitting. All those questions, I deceive myself each time; all those questions must mean that I have a chance. And so, I stay on, eventually serving myself forth like a scrawny roast pig only to be told "thank you, but no thank you."

"Thank you? Thank you? You should applaud! A standing ovation would not be inappropriate," I think each time. "I've just given you a story filled with exotic locales, travel on the open seas, family secrets, un-Christian vices. Thank you, will not suffice."

My self-righteous rage burns until I am forced to concede that I, in fact, have told them nothing. This language that I dip into like a dry inkwell has failed me. It made me take flight with weak wings and watched me plummet into silence. I am unable to tell them anything but a list of cities; some they've been to and others a mere dot on a globe, places they'll only touch with the tips of their fingers and never the soles of their feet. I am forced to admit that I am, to them, nothing but a series of destinations with no meaningful expanses in between.

"Thank you. But no thank you."

The third type, I call the "collectors." They are always good for several weeks and sometimes even several months worth of work. The interviews they conduct are professional, even mechanical. Before I can offer the usual inarticulate boast about my "good omelettes," I am hired. Breakfast, lunch and dinner to be prepared six days a week. Sundays off. Some immediately delegate the marketing to me. Others insist on accompanying me for the first week to make sure that I know the difference between a "poularde" and a "poulette."

I rarely fail them. Oh, of course, I have never been able to memorize nor keep an accurate tally of the obsessive assortment of words that the French have devised for this animal that is the center, the stewed, fricasseed, sautéed, stuffed heart, of every Frenchman's home. Fat chickens, young chickens, newly-hatched chickens, old wiry chickens...all are awarded with their very own name, a noble title of sorts, in this language, which can afford to be so drunk and extravagant towards what lies on the dinner table.

"A chicken" and "Not this chicken." These are the only words I need to navigate the poultry markets of this city. Communicating in the negative is not the quickest and certainly not the most esteemed form of expression, but for those with few words to spare it is the magic spell, the incantation which opens up an otherwise inaccessible treasure trove. Wielding my words like a rusty kitchen knife, I can ask for, reject, and ultimately locate that precise specimen which will grace tonight's pot.

And yes, for every coarse, misshapen phrase, for every blundered, dislocated word, I pay a fee. A man with a borrowed, ill-fitting tongue, I cannot compete for this city's attention. I cannot participate in the lively lover's quarrel between it and its inhabitants. I am a man whose voice is a harsh whisper in a city which loves a melody. No longer able to trust the sound of my own voice, I carry a small speckled mirror which shows me my face, my hands, and assures me that I am still here.

Becoming more animal-like with each displaced day, I scramble to seek shelter in the kitchens of those who will take me. Every kitchen is a homecoming, a respite, where I am the village elder, sage and revered. Every kitchen is a familiar story that I can relate and embellish with saffron, cardamom, bay laurel, and lavender. In their heat and in their steam, I allow myself to believe that it is the sheer speed of your hands, the flawless measurement of your eyes, the science of your tongue, that is rewarded. During these restorative intervals, I am no longer the mute who begs at this city's steps. Three times a day, I orchestrate and they sit with slacken jaws. Silenced. Mouths preoccupied with the taste of foods so familiar, and yet with every bite even the most parochial of palates detect redolent notes of something which they have no words to describe. They are, by the end, overwhelmed by an emotion which they do not know, a nostalgia for places they've never been.

I never willingly depart these havens. I am content to grow old in them, calling the stove my lover, calling the copper pans my children. But "collectors" are never satiated by my cooking. They are ravenous and compulsive. The honey that they covet lies inside my scars.

They are subtle in their tactics. A question slipped in with the money for the weekly food budget. A follow-up twisted inside a compliment for last night's dessert. Three others disguised as curiosity about the recipe for yesterday's soup. In the end, they are indistinguishable from the type-twos except for the defining core of their obsession. They have no interest in where I have been or what I have seen. They crave the fruits of exile, the bitter juices and the heavy hearts. They yearn for a taste of the pure, sea salt sadness of the outcast whom they've brought into their homes. And I am but one within a long line of others. The Algerian who was orphaned by a famine, the Turkish girl violated by her uncle, the Pakistani driven out of his village because his shriveled left hand was a sign of his mother's misdeeds. These are the wounded trophies who have preceded me.

It is not that I am unwilling. I've sold myself in exchange for less. Under their gentle guidance, their velvet questions, even I can disgorge enough pathos and cheap souvenir tragedies to sustain them. They are never gluttonous in their desires, rather the opposite. Methodical. A measured, controlled dosage is part of the thrill.

No, I am driven out by my own willful hands. Yes, it is only a matter of time. After so many weeks of having that steady, soft light shined at me, I begin to forget the demarcations, the barbed-wire rules of such engagements. I forget that there will be days when it is I who will have the craving, the red raw need to expose all my neglected, unkempt days. And I forget that I will wait, like a supplicant at the temple's gate, until all the rooms of the house are somber and silent.

When I am abandoned by their sweet-voiced catechism, I forget how long to braise the ribs of beef, whether chicken is best steamed over wine or broth, where to buy the sweetest trout...I neglect the pinch of cumin, the sprinkling of lovage, the scent of lime. And, in these ways, I compulsively write, page by page, the letters of my resignation.

Slow Tribe

Linh Dinh

They are the usual three:
One, who fantasizes about my death;
One, who craves my sex;
And one, who claims to be restless.
They come, singly, at odd intervals, unannounced,
Bearing exaggerated miens and inexpensive gifts:
Plastic flowers, slurs, bits of lint, leftover food.
They pick fights amongst themselves whenever they meet,
Or else they fuck on my bed, forgetting where they are.
I never ask them to leave, although I despise
Each one of them. They are my kin:
I, too, fantasize, claim to be restless, crave my own sex.

Lost and Found

Truong Tran

only a boy and still you were punished sent with a can forced to wear a bamboo
basket your hat sent to collect a father's humility a mother's shame in the form of
salt house to house door to door spoon to spoon a can full of salt for daily
consumption its taste on your tongue to serve as a reminder this a child's crime
waking to a wet bed

she says she saw you in a dream walking with a woman your father found a girlfriend changes her mind after a minute or so actually they're just friends she likes talking to the picture of you in the backyard beneath cherry blossoms the shadow of a branch hiding your smile she says of her children I have your temper throwing food at the cabinets breaking bowls in the kitchen she finds comfort in cleaning together without words I sweep the floors she washes the cupboards fated I was born the third of three brothers one the reflection I ran from the other a reminder of my hopes projected lost to be found only to lose again as a child I wanted a baseball bat a spherical object to hit without breaking windows in a house where fated I was born herself she wears tangerine peel thick to the bones and all the moons melt fingers toes between and through I who with but one iris is this boy she whispers in a way with charcoal teeth hisbiscus eyes paper frogs from finger she springs this boy is who she is in a way whispers it is I it is I

Sounding Sadec

Mộng Lan

> *The world was huge and complex yet very clear.*
> —*Marguerite Duras*

Shock of body against shock of land and sea—
M.D.   I've traveled to Sadec to find you:
                    I've airplained across the huge and clear Pacific
stretching imaginary like mathematics
                            I've many times ferried across the Mekong
an onerous expanse of oblivion and poverty
        and listened to it
and wept—
I find the primary school soybean-gold with lucid blue trimmings
where your mother taught
and today school is letting out early for a patriotic
holiday: hordes of mothers and fathers
perched intent
on their seats to motorcycle their children home—they could be waiting
                    waiting waiting
for Christ or the Buddha himself
                    to materialize
            from dust

when I see a Chinese-styled mansion from afar ornate
with painted story-telling tiles   I think
this must have been an important place
and it still is   the government has transformed it into
a police station   you can see four or five policemen
with their feet propped up on the table playing cards
my guide tells me this was where *the lover* lived
and this the lover's father's palace (he was the mandarin of Sadec)
I don't know if I should believe her   though the palace (not *blue* blue)
is facing the Mekong   and under the police station sign
they've another prohibiting photos

as luck would have it (or sheer will)
I see your ghost as a child
in a simple white dress walking
by that house   next to that familiar branch of the Mekong
and I can hear your high heels clacking
stares trailing behind you like clanking cans

in Vinh Long   I see you sipping jasmine tea
next to the silvery Mekong
a nova slides down the whispering sky
slipping into the Mekong like an oar—
all this a precursor
to your drunken stupor in later life?

Sadec   dusty provincial town in the South
a town like the others   but here every cell
         of my body is tracing your past
(where Indochina's mist has fashioned you bird-boned
                    North America's dreams
have steeped my marrow with thickness)
your childhood movements emblazoned in shift
         of air guides me,
marrow in my body
         to stillness of song
rapture of humble people rupture of proud lives
         in everything

that tells of the past   your past our present:
         rank bickering marketplaces
rusty ferries with their thunderous prewar motor
                    old brick factories like large domed ant hills
where inside adolescent girls dig into the earth
              clay gloves up to their chins
sun-wizened men and women watching
the spirit of the old Mekong
              unchanged   unchanging

one month later in Hanoi   I hear on the Vietnamese
national news that you've passed
         passed away in France   and your whole complex
              life
in a syncopated instant
                    tangos before me.

Nobody Knows

Quang Bao

[Author's Note: When I informed the characters in this story that I was applying, retroactively, a microphone and microscope to the day of November 17, 1996, they shot back, immediately, that while both of them would love to see themselves in print, it would appear more modest if I changed their names, slightly, to give readers only a vague idea of who or what the story might be about. The female lead made two appearances by telephone. The father, whose visit prompted the story, subsequently threatened to remove his only son from his will if the story were ever published, but that if it were, God help the family, to alter the color of his hairpiece (if it needed mentioning at all) from a heavy black to a light brown, having settled into a more suitable style.]

"What a lovely apartment!" my father shrieked, entering through the back door of my apartment. "Is this your room?" He deposited a duffel bag in what was actually a guest room in a two-bedroom apartment. "This is wonderful." He petted an engraved box in which I kept old letters. "Your room is clean, a bit on the small side, but nobody will know if you keep the door mostly closed." He strolled through the apartment, hands clasped behind his back, a usual disposition that marked his entrance into unfamiliar places where the possibilities for interior renovations seemed endless to him.

"Yeah, so, anybody who was anybody back then was there," he said, pouring himself a glass of water and walking into the living room. "I'm so glad I went. The wine had a wonderful bouquet, not a lot of cork, either." He swirled the glass around and took a sip, settling down on the living room couch.

During the ride back from the airport, my father was describing a reunion he had just attended in California of former military admirals from Vietnam. The affair, by his account, was no less than grand, which meant empty firing rifles mounted on the walls, a centerpiece ice sculpture of a military academy at the head table where he sat, a buffet spread of ladyfinger sandwiches, and a beautiful

Vietnamese girl playing on the piano a lovely Schubert piece, or maybe Handel—whatever it was, it was definitely lovely, he thought.

He reminisced, dragging me though an essentially plotless evening, from A to B, feeling it necessary to go through L, M, N, and even X, first, and not necessarily in that order. When he paused for water, I spoke up, in a detached voice that seemed to come out from one of the stereo speakers. "Dad, I have something I want to confess about myself, make clear rather, while you're sitting here," I stated.

Quickly, but somewhat effortlessly, he set the glass down onto the glass coffee table and fell back into the sofa. He rearranged some pillows into a fortress to protect himself from wherever the conversation happened to veer next. It was as if a close relative were about to tell him, officially, that all those accounts he had been hearing about the fall of South Vietnam were true, accounts which his mind had blocked out up until now and tossed aside as rumors and the work of conspirators and journalists. Very suddenly, his face let go of its usual blank expression—he had a plan—and contorted itself into a minimally pained grimace, like that of someone who has just bitten into a rotten plum, which looked deceptively unbruised on the surface. Agitatedly, he shot up from the comfortable loveseat and fell to the floor.

It was like a dream, or, more accurately, I had already dreamt this scene in which I was witnessing my father's collapse, only I couldn't remember what I did next because the dream usually climaxed here. By the time I decided what to do and made it over to where he was lying, twenty-five years seemed to have passed. I fitted my hands under his armpits and flipped him onto his backside so that he lay face up. And then the phone rang.

"Hello, San Francisco, this is your mother calling."

"Mom, Dad's lying again on—"

"Your father tells lies all the—"

"He's on the living room floor," I reported.

"Oh, dear," my mother said, changing the telephone from one ear to the other, "just what I need."

Two years ago, just around the time he learned of his impotency, my father invented a habit of orchestrating fainting spells. He made very little effort to be convincing, in manner and timing, sometimes even crossing hideously clustered spaces first to avoid any superficial injury to himself on his way down.

"Honey, your father is getting older," my mother said. "Just finish that Master's, give him a grandchild, and do whatever it is you keep writing about in those stories you keep sending us."

The stories were actually wordy, confessional letters I was mailing home regularly to my parents, who admired the "fictional sounding" aspects of the writing and the main character. They suggested sending the stories off to some well-circulated journal I had never heard of that also printed cooking recipes.

"They are not stories," I stressed. "They are letters, a-b-c-d-e-f-g, letters, facts about your son's l-i-f-e-s-t-y—"

"Where's your father now?" she broke in.

"He's still prostrate," I said.

She gasped. "I don't like all these puns and spelling games."

"Mother, why are you calling?"

"I wanted to ask your father something, but he's obviously predisposed so I won't bother," she said. "He hasn't told you anything yet?"

"I can't recall anything terribly newsy," I said.

"You and details," she said. "You're just like your—oh, honey, I've got a call on the other line. Can we talk more later?"

By now, a fly had landed on the bulb of my father's nose. The fly skipped and disappeared somewhere in his brownish-colored hair. I walked over and sat down perpendicularly to my father, supporting myself by leaning back on the palms of my hands. I stretched out my legs and slid my big toe underneath one of his belt loops and noticed a dry-cleaning tag still stuck to the safety pin on the inside waist of his trousers. I supposed telling your parents about the important things and people in your life outweighed the need to tell them under the ideal circumstances. To be honest, I was relishing the chance at an uninterrupted monologue and began telling my father about the four-year relationship I had been carrying on, when his eyes immediately reopened and he came to.

When my father was sitting back and upright on the couch, I looked at my watch (5:20 p.m.) and calculated that he had been in the apartment for approximately thirty-five minutes. He had repositioned himself safely behind an arrangement of throw pillows, the same way he was when he first entered the room.

"Mom just called," I said finally. "She said you were supposed to tell me something."

"Son, I don't know how you're going to take this," he sighed, pulling one of the pillows in closer. "Your mother and I would like you to find a wife, are considering a divorce ourselves, and, separately, I'm considering rhinoplasty."

The first two pieces of information had been debated, with increasing frequency and volume, over the past few years, and could hardly be considered new. The rhinoplasty, however, belonged on page one, conjuring up an image of something big and plastic that my father wanted fastened to himself.

"Neither of you has enough money to live apart," I pointed out. "We've done the math already. You've been together too long to separate anyway."

"Well, you needn't worry about the money part," he said. "The truth is that your mother doesn't know who I am anymore. She tripped over me the other day, or maybe I tripped her. Whatever. She apologized to the floor lamp, or the ottoman, or someone like that. I mean, I'm old, yes, but I'm not gone yet."   He pulled his hand out from one of the pillows and scratched the stubble on his chin.

I'd noticed that when other men grew older, they started looking wiser. And through some generous bending of Punnet-square rules, a forgivable phenotype made their aged faces more interesting and complex, an unannotated, scribbled-all-over tabula rasa, from which some of the most character-building experiences in life—marriage, war, death—could be downloaded on sight. My father's face seemed to have missed the wind-swept mayhem of aging. The only giveaway of his age could be located in his eyes. They were tiny, and the lids so amazingly wrinkled and overworked that I wondered if the irises could still filter the light amidst all of the erosion. With just that outstanding exception, his face looked the same as it did in a lineup photo of him at age twenty-four, a placid army cadet ready to be captured and pumped for information he didn't have.

I examined his nose closely. The organ was as long and rectangularish as possible, creating a visual speed bump in what would otherwise have been just an oval-shaped, trafficless layout of flesh, moles, and the normally spaced facial protuberances. I remembered when my father and I were waiting in the foyer inside the enormous three-story house of my horrific first date and how nervous I was. To prevent me from making a scene, he distracted me by trying to locate where exactly my date's bedroom was through a recreation of the entire floor plan, based on the odors he sensed coming out of different rooms. He was on a par with those who could discriminate differences in classical music or etchings. My father recognized the world only because he could smell it, and that, for him, was as close as he could get to understanding it.

"Dad, why on earth do you want a new nose?" I asked.

"Let's talk about you," he said, pointing a finger. "In Vietnam, men your age are all married or thinking about being married. Even Truc Vanh in that famous autobiography was at least seriously considering it." My father was always making obscure-sounding cultural allusions that were virtually impossible to verify. "Find someone, that's an order. And if you can't, come home this summer and your mother and I will help. Who knows?"

"Help?"

"I know a Vietnamese couple with a young mechanical engineer daughter," he said. "She's been to Paris, like you. The family's related to Balzac, I hear."

"Well, that's sufficient," I said. "I'd like to marry her, but some time in between my final exams and our first child, I'd like to have an affair, preferably with a semi-younger Vietnamese woman who owns a restaurant and likes to wear high—"

"Don't change the subject again!" he interrupted, shooting out from behind the pillow cushions. "This is about you, not anybody else. In Vietnam, you'd be cast out of society, a stranger, an aberration...no twenty-five-year-old man— you'd have to get your own apartment even!" Suddenly, his eyes started jumping around the room. "I could set something up for you easily. I'm a great match-maker! I've matchmade a whole bunch of people!"

"Who?" I cross-examined.

"At least five," he said, stretching out all five fingers on his left hand.

"That means ten actually, right?"

"Ten, even," he said, holding out the other hand. "Yes, of course, five times two is ten!"

"Brilliant," I said.

The phone rang again. He plopped back down to the sofa, and I let the answering machine pick up the call.

"Hi, honey, this is just Mom again," the voice said. "I want to get my two cents in before your father regains consciousness. I don't know what he's told you already but he's making up half of it and the other half he doesn't know what he's talking about, except for the fact that we would both love to marry you off and be done with the whole matter. Nobody's getting any younger around here, especially not me. This is long distance, so I won't be long, but could you just please stop telling the world about your feelings and just calm down a bit. I'm sure I speak for your father when I say that one out of seven women is Chinese, for heaven's sake, and why, I don't see how someone can't *not* find one woman with those kinds of odds. We were oppressed and everything by the Chinese, I think, but that was so long ago I can hardly remember it. I wouldn't necessarily mind—"

My father, having crossed the room, snatched the phone off its cradle.

"We're both here," he announced. "You've said enough for all of us already so why don't you just—" He paused and then covered his hand over the mouthpiece. "She wants to talk to you." I waved my hand back and forth to both of them. "You see, he doesn't even want to talk to you anymore," he said, back into the telephone. "Honestly, nagging us all to death isn't—" He abruptly stopped again, walked with the telephone into the kitchen, and shut the door for privacy.

Once they stopped arguing, I could overhear fragments of a ploy to get me to concede and see things their way: a newly designed house, built just down the street from my parents, with all the modern conveniences installed; inside, a twisted staircase that uncoiled eventually to the master bedroom door, half-opened to reveal a resplendently dressed bed, draped in sheets of satin, on which my new Vietnamese bride was just about to lie—"The war is over, honey, come to bed."

from **Rosary**

Barbara Tran

Do I begin at the here and now,
or does the story start
with the first time
my mother took the wheel—
the first woman to drive
in a country where men
are afraid to walk?

My mother's story begins
when the steam rises.
It ends when it's ready.
Taste it. Does it need more salt?

Heat

Today, at sixty-seven, she stands at the stove at work. The heat overcomes her. She thinks she is standing at the shore. The steam is like a warm breeze being carried out to sea. My mother hears the seagulls circling above. She feels the sun on her skin and admires the reflection on all the shining fish bodies. Her father's men have been collecting the nets for days now, laying the fish out for fermenting. The gull with the pure white underside swoops toward the fish farthest away, lands on an overturned boat, its sides beaten and worn, its bottom sunburned like a toddler's face after her first day of work in the rice fields. Beside the boat, a palm hut, where the fishermen hang their shirts, and where their wives change when it's time for a break from the scooping and jarring, when their black pants become hot as the sand itself. And then the laughter starts, and the women's bodies uncurl from their stooped positions, their pointed hats falling back, the men treading anxiously in the water as they imagine a ribbon pulling gently at each soft chin.

Bait

Through the eye, my grandfather threads the rusty hook, forces it back through the body of the fish. The tail curves around as if frozen mid-leap. The seagulls never leave. The smell of fish always in the air. Today, the old man will give them nothing. It is his daughter he is thinking of. My mother is fourteen and beginning to turn heads. Her father thinks she will like the seagull with the pure white underside. He watches the birds, daring one another to come closer. He watches the younger ones in their confusion. The swoop and retreat. He has not fed them for days. Minutes go by, and he thinks the boats will come in soon, scattering the gulls. The Year of the Snake is only days away. He would buy his daughter a dove, but she likes the wind. With a quick swoop, a gull grabs the fish in its beak. The old man wraps the line around his roughened hands, braces himself for the tug, as the line grows more taut. And suddenly the bird jerks in the sky, wings extended as if it's been shot.

Cage

Easter lilies spill from her thin arms. The flowers and her gloves equally as spotless. This is how it began. My mother would never forget the seagull with the hook through its bill. Often she would recall how wrong the imagination could go. All she had been thinking about was the pure white of its underside. Not the high-pitched cry of a child being separated from all it knows. The best part was seeing it finally take to its wings again. It was still in the cage that her father built, but she could pretend it had its freedom. It could fly higher than she could reach.

Downpour

She knew it was coming by the way the glass jars shook in the darkness, the occasional flash of lightning, crawling the walls like quick lizards. A rain so heavy, things would be hammered into the earth. She thought of all the glass jars resting on their shelves, all the hours the men spent, blowing these cylinders for the *nuoc mam* they made from the anchovies they caught, and then, the few drinking glasses they made for themselves on the side when her father wasn't watching. After the rain, the broken pieces would once again have to be melted down and mixed together. And here, her father lay in bed, smoking away the profits. With each breath in, the fishing boats moved farther and farther away. With each breath out, more jars needed to be made, sold. Her father couldn't even hear the thunder. The lightning, warm flashes on his lids, like the sun when he was trying to nap in the afternoon. He thought the glassblowers earned him a puff on his pipe with each puff on theirs. He should reap the rewards of being an old man, of owning his own fishery. But with each breath, his daughter grows more impossibly beautiful. He knows he will not be able to keep her long.

Safe

The three sisters sip their tea, try to hold their tongues, as she uncovers the safe. Marie piles the bars of gold to the side, and pulls out a sack of bills, grabs two bundles, and puts the rest back. She covers the safe with the red cloth as before, bowing to the picture of her grandmother. The women think of their brother in Saigon, playing poker in his white jacket, his slicked back hair. They think of the young girls he has loved, the angry parents they have faced. Then they think of him married to Tran Thi Marie, driving her father's Mercedes. They remember her grandfather and his plot of banana trees, the fruit drying in the sun. They have seen her father's fishing fleet. They think of the meals they will have whenever they visit their brother. Marie is a gorgeous woman. They will tell their mother.

Faith

For years, my grandfather thought he could keep my mother by his side. She seemed content with her prayers and fasting. But he didn't know about the couple that sat before her at Mass that Sunday morning. She had noticed them, the man sitting next to the woman as if she were any other. But then, the stolen glances, the passing of a prayer book, the spreading of goose bumps, from the neck down the arms, the woman crossing herself.

The first time my father saw my mother, she was driving the barren countryside of Bien Ho. How vain, he thought to himself: wearing Easter lilies in her hair. What he didn't know was that they actually were Easter lilies, she was on her way to Mass. She wore them year-round to remind herself that Jesus was always risen—if you kept Him alive in your life.

Proof
They were married before her father knew it,
her father smoking opium in the bright sun.
All he could remember
was the white jacket, the black tie,
the boat rocking, the boys reaching,
dragging the net.
The net full of fish.
The fish drying in the sun.
The seagulls swarming like men
honing in on the scent.
The slow peeling of an orange.
Smoke coming from his pipe.
The juice squirting.
The spewing out of pits.
And then, she was packing.

Prayer
My grandfather had always had three women in the kitchen, someone continuously preparing something. Fresh bread, hot banana pudding, sweet rice with coconut. And now his daughter was leaving, and the women were selecting china for her to take. He wondered how this happened. She was the last of his daughters, and he had spoiled her, hoping to keep her for himself. For years, he spent his days, from the moment he woke until the sun began its slow dive into the water, submerged, working the fishing nets, his skin puckered like a mango left in the sun too long. And here, his daughter would still need to watch the gills heave up and down, the gasping at the small mouth. Still, she'd need to chop the head off, blood running down the sides of the cutting board, her hands covered with

scales. For years, he tried to keep her hands from coming in contact with anything but the food she ate and the money she counted. Now they would be roasted daily over a fire.

He wondered how crowded her new home would be, how long she would have to live with her in-laws, how such a small child would bear a child. He knew she would find it difficult to breathe in the smog-filled streets of Saigon. He closed the trunk for her, knelt down beside her, pressed a bar of gold into her palm. He wanted her to write as often as possible. She nodded. She wanted to stay, to hold her father's hand, to watch the fishing boats come in, to listen to the seagulls like hungry beggars outside.

Hope

It all began with her driving the barren country roads, barren because the men were too fearful to walk them. Knife-blade to the neck, my mother still refused to hand over the pearls her father gave her for her first Christmas as a teen, as a target for unmarried men. Really, what she hoped they wouldn't find was the pearl rosary her mother left behind. She felt the blade bite deeper into her neck: the same place her husband would often bite her the first year they were married, the last year she would think of love as something shared between two people. After the first child, she would think of duty and responsibility and mirrors. She cared for herself and so, her child. Love remained between her and God. Husbands were meant to be fathers, children to be married off. Her mother's rosary was proof she agreed. The cross was melded from her wedding ring. It was crooked from being slammed in the door as she ran from her husband. One day my mother would hide the same beads beneath her pillow, as if to ward her own husband away, as if after seven children, he might somehow stop.

Hunger

In Saigon, a daughter on each hip, she began to wonder where the rice was going. Leaving one child home sucking her thumb, the other holding her empty belly, my mother hailed a taxi. In front of the cathedral, the pink nails in the car ahead crept across the man's neck, and she recognized both. This was, after all, the man who woke her body. Before him, she knew only the ache of chopping and carrying, of balancing heavy loads. Now there was a different kind of pull, like the sea, and after it, a different kind of heavy load, filling her belly. Of course, she followed him.

* * *

Balance

On the way back from the market each day, the pole teeters across her back, a pot on either side. The one on the right, emptied of its *pho*; the one on the left, full of dirty bowls and the leftover dishwater she was too impatient to drain. Cuong skips ahead, his short hair bouncing with each step. She quickens and grabs her youngest son's ear, twisting it, not because he is getting too far ahead, or because he is daydreaming, but because she can't. Her husband gone with the two oldest children, my mother still has four. He lives in a duplex in Manhattan; she sells *pho* for ten cents a bowl and needs someone to hold. Cuong is getting too big, with his slingshots and firecrackers, his patched eye from Tet. Each day she drags my grandmother's bed a little closer to hers, brings a mirror along with dinner to her mother's bedside.

Measure

My mother's recipes are not even close to precise. Everything is in approximate proportion. One portion of *nuoc mam* to three of water and one of vinegar, some lime, a big pour of sugar. Maybe some more. This is in opposition to her determination to keep my father. With this, she was painfully methodical.

When she got off the plane, rosary wound around her left hand, her right dragging Cuong along, did she think about the child growing inside her? I was not yet growing inside her, but she knew I would be soon. She knew also that there was a child growing inside some other woman's womb, and that it would be born first, and that her husband would be there. Still, she had four children in tow, all of whom would cry out "Ba!" on cue. They had had enough rice with *canh* for dinner. Now they were in the United States of America, with all its independence and escalators, its planes, trains, and fast ways of getting away. They weren't letting go.

Epilogue

Brush stroke number forty-nine
and her hair shines like a black cat's.
She can think of nothing
but the days when she wore her hair
above her shoulders, moved her hips
like a boy. And still the men
couldn't help but look. Now
there are so many things
to fit into the frying pan:
the daughter with the red
lingerie rolled inside her dirty
school uniform, the son
with the twisted jaw
and the constant longing
for a cold beer, the husband
she chased in taxicabs,
holding her extended belly
only to finally say, Please,
take me home. At seventeen,
my mother counted her Hail Marys
on the little white beads
of her rosary. Now she counts them off
on the heads of her seven children,
counting herself as eight,
and her husband,
as one and ten.

A Pressing Romance

Diep Khac Tran

I watched you spend a summer teaching
my hands to print; afternoons in pools
of discarded scraps of text from this
business of papers, inks, and types. Nights,
I took the words and set in your room
my own galley of ruined type held
bound with wood and metal blocks, coated
in a fortune of ink. Your intent
forgotten, September produced no
paper reliefs, but an embossed back—
my printer's proof from a summer long
in lessons. You covered up your press
and resigned that I soon will tire
myself of autobiography.

Fritz Glatman

by Linh Dinh

Mariechelle, Norie, Loida, Sylvana, Emie, Dulce, Maria, Marites .... The catalog, Origami Geishas, is laid-out like the cheapest high school yearbook. Twenty-four out-of-focus black and white photographs to a newsprint page. Thirty-two pages. Six-hundred-plus brown women desiring a white man who will take her into his home.

LBFM-168 Geniva (19) Philippines/5-3; 103; domestic helper (some college) "Frankly I long for male friend with no vice, a strong sense of humour, believe in Our Saviour. I am kind-hearted, simple-minded and sincere. I like bowling."

LBFM-352 Consorcia (28) Malaysia (Filipina)/4-10; 95; Agri-forester/zoologist; "I like soft music, Thoreau, dancing, cooking. I like a man who is easy to go along, no back talking. I am interested in soul mates, some drinking, not too much."

LBFM-577 Goldnar (21) Hong Kong (Filipina)/5-0; 100; student; Catholic. "I am lovable."

I am Fritz Glatman (43), American, of English and Austrian extractions/6-1; 227 lbs; Of Counsel at the Center City law firm of Gontarek & Enfield. I am divorced, with no children. My ex, Jane Kulik, was recently made a partner at Cohen, Javens, Petaccia & Kulik. We've been exchanging Christmas cards every year for the past 14 years.

Within the past year I've been toying with the idea of securing for myself an Asian woman, a mail-order bride. I've been brooding over this prospect, sober or drunk, on many sleepless nights. A hoary wet dream, I'd think, emitting a little laugh. A last ditch recourse. Aegri somnia.

This solution plunged me into the deepest shame initially, but I am now increasingly resigned to its feasibility. There's even a dull excitement daily creeping up on me.

Before this idée fixe, if you will, took hold, I was never partial to Asian women. Never even thought about them. But with mental exertion came a gradual, grudging appreciation. Stare at anything long enough, I suppose, and beauty will rise to the surface.

The girls in Origami Geishas are mostly plain, their faces plain, their hair plain. Some are outright ugly. But my future wife must be unequivocally beautiful, though not too beautiful. Son of an immigrant, I was taught to be modest, to shy away from luxuries, and to shun all ostentatious displays. Indeed, even with a six-figure salary, I drive an old-modeled Ford.

But I should quantify that she must be at least several notches better looking than I am. Like any man, I cannot be satisfied with merely an equitable return for my pecuniary investment. I want a little extra.

She need not be too smart, obviously. If I want to feed my brain, I'll buy a book. What it comes down to is this: I can only exchange what I have, money, and the fact that I'm a citizen of a First World country, for what she has, what every woman has.

My wife will undoubtedly be a social incongruity in my life, a foul ball and a blip on my record. I'm a lawyer, not a sailor for Uncle Sam. But since it would not be feasible to conceal her existence from my colleagues, to lock her up, figuratively speaking, in a carriage house or a wine cellar, sentence her to life without parole, or to introduce her as an au pair—or, rather, as a maid—to my neighbors, I must steel myself for the negative publicity, from the invidious snickers to righteous smirks to actionable slanders. Caveat emptor.

To facilitate her assimilation into this society, perhaps it is advisable that I send her to the Community College for a semester or two of remedial English, art and music appreciation, and to let her wallow in the secure ambience of a college campus.

My father, long dead, would not have objected to my marrying an Asian woman. A kind-hearted, simple-minded and sincere man, he was a concrete contractor for 40-odd years, specializing in driveways, patios, handicapped ramps, and stucco. Although he never finished high school, he was an enthusiastic reader. He pronounced "Orientals" "Orienals." He would lecture to his five children: "The Orienals are an inward people. I have a lot of respect for them. They have an inward orienation because of their physiognomy. The epicanthic folds on their eyes block out much of the sun, and hence much of the world. They have a wispy physique, and do not gorge themselves on red meat like we do. They live on top of each other, in gross discomfort, which drives them further inward. They live close to the earth, build flat houses, and are small of stature."

He had a peculiar concept called "perpendicularity." Angles and curves had to be minimized. All the furniture in our house, beds, tables, were lined up at a 90 degree angle to the wall, hugging it, with the middle of the floor kept empty. Thrown rugs were banished, since they could not be maintained at right angles. At dinner, forks and knives, when at rest, had to be placed perpendicular to the edge of the table. Likewise, if our chairs were not perpendicular to the edge of the table as we were eating, he would whack us on the head. Do not lean against the wall, he always reminded us. "The Orienals sit at round tables," he said. "They have no sense of perpendicularity."

A minor problem: I've been advised that the Filipinos cannot enunciate the "f" sound. They call their own country "Pilippines." It is perhaps the only country in the world which cannot pronounce its own name. Instead of "Fritz," my wife would have to call me "Pritz."

Naturally, in thinking about my future wife, I've become more alert to all things Asian. At least three times a week, you'll find me at some restaurant in Chinatown, happily stuffing my face with sashimis, happy pancakes, spring rolls or wontons. I'm conditioning my innards for her cooking. I asked Justin Park (née Duk Chong Park), a new associate at our firm, for book recommendations. We were standing by the Mr. Coffee: "Justin, I've been thinking a lot about Southeast Asia recently, the Philippines in particular. I want to take a trip there next year. Never been to Asia. Can you recommend me a book to read?"

"I'm Korean, Fritz."

"I know, buddy, I know! Duck Pork is a Korean name! Pusan City. I've seen your resume. But if anyone here knows anything about Asia, you do, so don't be so defensive."

"Alright, alright, there's a novel by Jessica Hagedorn called *Dogeaters*"

"*Dogeaters*?!"

"Yes, *Dogeaters*"

"Is it any good? What's it about?"

"It's pretty good," he furrowed his brows, tried to remember the book, "but it's hard to summarize it. There's too many characters. It's about Manila. There's a guy named Joey Sands, a half-black, half-Filipino hustler, and a fat German film director, a Fassbinder-type whom the hustler called 'Rain or Shine.'"

"That's pretty clever: Rainer, Rain or Shine!" He was trying to get back at me for being a Kraut, I could tell.

Justin has been with us for just over a year. Fresh from Harvard Law, he does fairly good work but is perceived by the other attorneys as being a tad too cocky. As the firm's first minority hire, however, his job is reasonably secure. He wears a loud tie not only on Fridays but on every other day as well. While standing in the elevator lobby, he would often shoot an invisible basketball at an invisible hoop, throw an invisible football at an invisible receiver, or swing an invisible bat at an invisible baseball. He would pull these stunts even in the presence of clients. But, in spite of this showy proclivity for sports, he declined to join our softball team. After he became adjusted to his new surrounding, as his confidence grew, he went out and got both of his ears pierced. He was sleeping with one of the temps, a petite 22 year-old named Traci Mintz, a clone of Shannon Miller, the gymnast who broke her ankle on TV. They were often seen leaving TGIF together. It is none of my business, of course, but our firm is fairly small, with only twelve attorneys.... After Traci left, he started to pork our beloved, long-time receptionist, Julia LaPorte, a buxom widow in her late 30's.

A week after our chat about the Philippines, Justin said: "Fritz, I don't mean to be nosy, but, ah, are you thinking about getting yourself a mail-order bride?"

I stared at him in disbelief. What chutzpah! Doesn't this punk know what privacy is? "Whoa! ha! ha! That's pretty funny. Why would you say that?"

"Just asking."

I looked him straight in the eyes, tried not to blink too fast: "I'm going to the Philippines because I want to see Asia: a guy like me, 43 years old, never seen Asia. It's the biggest continent in the world, you know, all those people, ha! ha! I can't afford Korea. Or Japan. Or Singapore. And Vietnam: all those bad associations. And I also have, uh, this interest in volcanoes. I grew up in Washington State, I don't know if you know that, near Mount St. Helen. She popped her top fifteen years ago, remember?" He was blank. "Maybe you weren't even here then. But there's this one spectacular volcano in the Philippines called, uh," I couldn't think of its damn name, "it's on the tip of my tongue. What is it, what is it, what's the name of that volcano?"

It was a dreadful performance, and I'm sure he saw right through me. Maybe I can figure out a way to get him fired before I bring my bride over.

Sitting in Chinatown restaurants, surrounded by Asians laughing and yakking away as they ate, I've come to realize that they are simply more forthright about life's amenities than we are. There is a recently released film directed by this Chinese guy, Ang Lee, called "Eat, Drink, Man, Woman." I didn't see the film, but I know what the title means: Eat, drink, man, woman.

Then there is this other film called "The Ballad of Nagasaki," by a guy named Arakawa. In it, there was this Japanese hick who had just lost his wife. The entire village helped him to find a new wife. She arrived from the next village, sight unseen. First thing she did was stuff her face with potatoes, she was starving, then she lay next to him. They had sex without saying a word to each other. Afterwards, he said: "I feel much better."

When I go to The Office, a go-go bar on 15th street, I see men from all over, a veritable assembly of the United Nations. Nowhere else can I hobnob so freely with Pakistanis, blacks and Mongolians. Each man nursing an unconsolable hard-on, wearing a shroud of pussies, we are all humbled, pared down, incorporated. We must all share the nude girl hanging upside down from the greased pole. She's presently doing a series of queer sit-ups to polite applause. None of us can have her. The best we can do is give her a dollar. It is the most democratic place on earth. The women, too, had come from all over the world. I'm reminded of a Cézanne painting called "The Eternal Female," in which men of various professions and pretensions, high and low, are depicted gazing up at a naked woman hovering over their heads.

Apropos of prostitution and pornography, a symbolic defilement of intimacy and a seance of lovemaking, respectively: I would never patronize a whore because I cannot consent to sex without commitment, with neither preface or prologue, but neither will I allow myself to be titillated, or moved to the depths of my soul, by a photo of a naked female, the cheapest form of idolatry. (Masturbation, which is unavoidable, I consider a breathing exercise, a cardiovascular fitness program and a jogging of the memory.) I avert my eyes from lingerie ads in the newspaper. If I must read an article on the same page as the ad, I cover the exposed flesh with a book or a bagel.

A remedy to the aforesaid perversions, of course, is the go-go bar. In front of me is a real woman, after all, doing what all women do, one way or another. She is alert to my presence, as I am to hers. We have a relationship. The slightest shift in mood in either party is duly registered by the other, a yawn, a pitying smile, a hardening of the facial features betraying irritation or disappointment.

The idea itself, of procuring a mail-order bride, can be traced to the fact that a friend of mine from undergraduate school married a Chinese woman two years ago. The pale pink wedding invitation arrived in the mail. Brian Panzram will be wedded to Josie Woo. I called Brian up. I said: "So, Brian, who's this Josie Woo?"

Then Lafcadio Kerns, an associate at our firm, showed up with a Thai girl at last year's Christmas party. She was much, much too beautiful for someone like Laffy, a squat fellow with a beer belly and eyes dilating in two directions. I was standing next to Justin by the hors d'oeuvres table. "Check out Laffy's squeeze," I said.

Justin crammed a slice of pâté-smeared bruschetta into his mouth, chewed it with his mouth open. "Yeah?"

"That's not right."

He chuckled, flushed his mouth with martini.

"Look at her!"

"Relax, Fritz."

"Look at him!"

"You think she's that hot?"

"Are you blind?!"

"She's alright."

"Every man should have a girl that pretty. How come you're not with a Chinese girl?"

"I would ask an Asian girl out for a date if I were white."

An odd thing for him to say, I thought. I even thought he had said: "I would ask an Asian girl out for a date if only I were white," but then that really wouldn't make any sense.

"And why do you care?" he continued.

"Never mind, never mind," I waved him off and walked away.

The music was vibrating the floor. I went to the bar and said: "Give me some of that Puligny whatever." The grinning bartender tilted the heavy bottle over my trembling flute. I drank it in one gulp, spilling half of it on my shirt. It's time to leave, I decided.

I sidled along the wall, dodging the tuxedoed and black-dressed figures convulsing to the techno music. This ape-din, why do people listen to it?

I almost made it to the door when Laffy intercepted me: "Yo, Fritz!" He was hoisting a bottle of Cristal over his nearly-bald head, spilling champagne all over it, a drunken gloat. One of his hands appeared surgically sewn to his girlfriend's bare midriff.

"I've got to go. I've got to go." I tried to ward him off.

"I'd like you to meet Grace."

"Nice to meet you, Grace," I extended my hand, "I'm Fritz Glatman."

"I'm Grace."

"Grace what?"

"Grace Kittikasem."

"What's that? Thai?"

"Very good," she said, with discernible disdain in her voice. If only we were alone, you fuckin' bitch, I'd teach you some American manners. Laffy was frowning at me, his eyes dilating in two directions. It was all I could do to refrain myself from punching him in the face.

Pre-Dahmer

Trac Vu

The first time I ever chewed gum, it was in Sai Gon after the communists took over. Food was scarce. We were constantly hungry. My brother's friend's aunt abroad sent his family a shipment that contained a pack of Spearmint. Strawberry flavor or something like that. When my brother got back with the loot, it was late at night, a couple of hours after dinner, which we had stretched to no end: five people had shared an omelet made with two eggs and nineteen tomatoes. When I started chewing on the Spearmint, the sugar melted on my tongue. I wanted to swallow the gum right then and there, eat it. But I knew that I couldn't, that gum was for chewing, that eventually I'd have to spit it back out, in one piece. That's what it was like sucking a guy for the first time.

Tale of Apricot

Minh Duc Nguyen

I wake up this morning and feel no different than when I went to sleep. For hours, I lie here and observe the branches of the apricot tree that I slept under. I have recently made a promise not to sleep under any tree more than once. This third tree, so far, has the most complicated structure to remember.

I get up and wander around the apricot orchard. These days I have a lot of free time. And I don't have any friends left. They either died or disappeared some time ago. But I'm too old to need friends. The only face that I can remember anyway is that of Chu Que. At times, I look at my hands like they are the young faces of me and him, and I watch them speak to each other. At other times, I just laugh with the crickets and roll around on the wild grass, and I hug the yellow sand by the creek and sleep with the fallen apricots. And slowly, I feel more and more like, what if, I am a ghost.

I can't help but walk toward the apricot cannery. From where I am, the cannery appears as a gray umbrella, shielding the workers inside from the harsh sun of Fresno. Beneath that faded roof, each family, mainly of mother and daughters, gathers around a long wooden table, slicing apricots in halves. They peel out the large brown seed inside the apricot and assemble the halves on a tray as large as the table. They stack one full tray on top of another. And at the end of each day, Mr. and Mrs. Best, the owners of this plantation, would give them two-fifty cash for each tray. Time is money, as people say, so they cut fast.

Inside the warehouse, I walk from one family to another. It is something that I have done for the past two days. I eavesdrop on their conversation but I keep my distance. I hear all kind of languages: Spanish, Chinese, Cambodian, Vietnamese, and more, but rarely English. The only time these workers would make an effort to speak English is when Mr. Best is around. But his tall frame is nowhere to be seen today. His wife, a small but attractive Chinese woman in her late thirties, is now chatting freely in her dialect among the Chinese families. Mrs. Best lets her dog, a black mutt with a stubby tail, skip around from one table to the next. The dumb dog jumps on everyone it sees and leaves prints of its dirty paws on their shirts.

"No, Vita! No!" Mrs. Best yells at her dog.

Briefly still, Vita stares back at its owner, confused. Then it runs away and resumes its bad manners.

I move toward the right wing of the cannery where all the Vietnamese families are concentrated, and I find the spot where I can be in the center of all of them. I hear that Mrs. Tan is giving Mrs. Anh tips on how to cook bun bo Hue without using MSG—just stew the beef back and tail bones in a large pot for three days to maximize the richness of the broth. Mrs. Nga is telling her daughter Linh not to go out with her boyfriend Minh any longer since he's not going to college. Mrs. Bich, probably the youngest mother there, is pregnant again. She wants a boy this time. Mrs. Thi, who stands in the corner, still hasn't said a word since I first saw her, but rumors tell me that her husband has left her for another woman. Mrs. Ha, a recent immigrant, complains that there aren't any good Vietnamese restaurants in Fresno, how the dishes that they make here are so plain, more like for the American healthy taste, and how the chicken meat here is too tender. She longs for egg noodles from Da Lat, fresh nuoc mam from Phu Quoc, longans from My Tho.

I stand here and listen to the Vietnamese that these families speak. Their words dance in my mind and it doesn't take many beats before I am back in Saigon.

I was three and was already wandering around the main streets day after day with Chu Que, my one-legged uncle, begging for spare change. Chu Que was not my blood relative but it didn't really matter because he was the only one who took care of me, and I didn't know how I came into existence anyway. He said he found me one night in a garbage can located in the back of a dog-meat restaurant. It was dark at the time he picked up my arm and thought that it was a dog bone with some skin left on it. I started to cry when he bit me, and Chu Que then thought that I was a dog with some horrible disease that the chef didn't want to cook and threw away half-killed. But when he saw my fingers grabbing tightly on his crutch, he knew right away that I was someone who had come into his life to fill in as his missing right leg. He lifted me out of the garbage can and into this world, and he bandaged my bleeding arm with a banana leaf. He found a rope and tightened one end around my neck and the other end on his crutch. And Chu Que called me Cho Con, his little dog, until he died.

I was lucky, Chu Que told me. My life could have been much worse. I could have been found by other beggars, perhaps a leper who would pass me his disease, and my hands and feet would have deteriorated when I reached ten, and I would have had to push my body around on a four-wheeled cart, or I could have been found by a desperate beggar who would have twisted my arms and legs and turned me into a freak—a showcase of pity to get more spare change. I asked Chu Que if that was what happened to him, that perhaps some beggars had kidnapped him from his family and broke off one of his legs. But Chu Que didn't say anything. To this day, I still don't know how he'd lost half of his right leg. Well anyway, at least with Chu Que, I still had all my body parts and grew up somewhat normally in the place I knew best. At least with him, I turned out somewhat a human being, or partly.

And standing here in the apricot cannery and in the middle of these families who speak my language, I am not asking for their pity. I am not asking for their spare change. I only seek their recognition that I have the same body parts as them, that I am a human being like them. I want them to see me, if not all of me, then parts of me.

Standing very close to me is little Trang. She has a dirty face even though the morning is still young. Her hands and slingshot are tucked deeply in her pant pockets. The rubber bands on the slingshot hang loose outside. She is standing around with nothing to do, so she decides to try her luck again.

"Ma," says Trang. "Can I help, please?"

Mrs. Ly and her oldest daughter Ngoc are busy with the apricots in their hands. The left hand holds the apricot with three fingers. The right hand holds the small knife with a short curve blade. The right thumb presses the sharp blade deep into the apricot. The three fingers on the left hand rotate the fruit, allowing the blade to slit along the groove that nature imprints on every apricot.

"I can do it, Ma. Let me show you." Little Trang sneaks her hand into Mrs. Ly's blouse pocket where she keeps the extra knife.

"Go away." Mrs. Ly pushes Trang's hand away. "You don't know how."

"Ma, I know how. It's like cutting apple."

"How many times have I told you that this is not an apple? This is an apricot, like a small peach. There's a large seed inside. You have to cut around it, and you have to cut right to get two equal halves. Otherwise, the lady boss will yell, understand? You don't know how. Now, go go, so I can work!"

Sister Ngoc feels pity for her much younger sister, so she says, "Trang, you can help me peel out the seed."

"I don't want to peel seed. I want to cut. Why don't you peel seed and I cut?"

Sister Ngoc smiles. "All right. Let me see if you can cut." And she is about to hand little Trang her knife, but Mrs. Ly stops her.

"No. I said she's too young to know how to cut. She'll cut her fingers instead. Girls with scars are ugly." Mrs. Ly rumbles on to explain that a girl's hands should be soft and white like steamed rice. The fingers should be long and somewhat fat where they meet the knuckles and pointed at the tips. But most importantly, the hands should be free of scars. If a hardworking girl has beautiful hands, it is a sign that she is kheo leo, clever, and she will know how to keep her house together when she has a family of her own. It's strange how Mrs. Ly's hands are nothing like what she described. Her frail hands appear used and dry around the finger tips. Red marks rest on her palms and long veins emerge through the brown skin. Perhaps they were once white and soft.

"Why don't you go play with the other kids?" Sister Ngoc tells little Trang, who is still staring at the knife. "Go go and come back later for lunch."

Finally, little Trang trots away toward the apricot orchard, kicking her feet high. She raises her hands and gazes at them. Her fingers clench into tight fists. I don't think she realizes how small her hands are.

I follow her. The poor girl must not think of herself as useless. I have a feeling she will do something of great importance for me.

I wish I could stop little Trang at this moment and talk to her and teach her the art of begging. All she had to do was to look deeply at her mother's hands with her light brown eyes and say, "Ma, you have beautiful hands." And I'm sure Mrs. Ly would soften and wrap her daughter's hands inside her own and they would cut together.

I knew all there was to know about begging. Chu Que taught me all the tricks, and I formulated some myself. The secret was to look like a beggar but talk like a poet.

"Cho Con, don't beg and they will give," said Chu Que. He often used breakfast as an example to show his point.

"It's early morning, and you are hungry and you want to eat breakfast. A man walks by. He's neither rich nor poor. Cho Con, what would you do?"

"Chu Que, I'd say, 'Chu a Chu, I'm hungry. Would you be kind and spare me some change?'"

"Well, that's not bad, Cho Con. You asked politely. And you look like a cute little girl, although very dirty. The man will pity you and give you two dong. With that, you can buy one Chinese donut for breakfast. But suppose you want more. Suppose you want a bowl of porridge with stuffed pork intestines to go with your donut. How do you convince this man to give you five more dong?"

"Hmmm?...I'll say that you are my father...and you are very sick...and...that I need money to go buy you medicine."

"Oh, Cho Con, you lie. That's very good. You're learning every day. But there's no need to lie unless it's a matter of life and death. And besides, what if I'm not with you? Who would be your father?"

"Chu Que, what would you do?"

"Now, listen. You're a little girl. People like little girls. It's early morning, a man walks by, you're hungry and want to eat breakfast. If you wave your hand at him, look him straight in the eyes, and greet him with a smile, just this much I'll guarantee you that most of the time the man will already give two dong so you can buy a Chinese donut. But now you want a bowl of porridge, so it's a little trickier. You'll have to play a game with the man. Nothing is for free, understand? You play a game with him and he'll pay you for it."

"What game, Chu Que?"

"A game of words. Man likes to play games to test his wit. It's his stupid nature. So you ask him a silly question that makes him think but he cannot answer...like...like 'Chu a Chu, do you know how big the moon is?' Hah, see? The man probably stops, thinks about it for a few seconds, and says, 'I really don't know. Why do you ask, little girl?' Now, this is when what you say counts the most! How much more the man will give you depends on how smart your answer is. You'd say something like this, 'Chu a Chu, last night I was so hungry that I couldn't sleep. So I laid here on the street awake all night and I watched the moon. The moon was so beautiful. It was bright, round and large, as large as your face! But I think the moon is probably much bigger than that. Chu a Chu, am I right?' What can he say now? Nothing! The man will nod his head in defeat. He'll pat you on the head and give you the extra five dong for your bowl of porridge, and he'll walk away smiling at his own kindness."

By the time I was seven, I had mastered this game of wit, which was played differently with a rich man or a poor man, young man or old man, a man or woman, tourists or local people. I rarely had to say "please" or even "spare change." But things became worse as I got older. I was no longer a cute little girl. I had to readjust and that was a new lesson. When I came to America, I encountered several beggars in San Francisco. They either sat in their corners and shook their paper cups with a few coins inside, or they just said, "Spare change?" And I laughed so hard at them.

Little Trang runs as fast as she can across the apricot orchard. She is anxious to meet the other children at the wild blackberry shrubs by the creek. But at halfway, her right foot steps into a squirrel's hole, and she falls down hard and scratches her left elbow on a sharp stone. Slowly, little Trang sits up. She holds her bleeding elbow close to her face and observes her wound carefully, with admiration. Then, with her fingertips, she rubs saliva off her tongue and cleans her wound. The touch of saliva on her injury must have created a burning pain, for her left cheek twitches continuously. But she remains still and quiet. The blood on the round scrape, which seems redder than a Tet good luck money envelope, soon clots in the dry summer heat. In a week, she'll have a new scar, and she'll have to hide it from her mother. The girl stands up on her feet. She kicks the dirt off her pants. As if she's forgotten about her fall, she races toward the creek, as fast as she can, like a wild mustang.

I run after her.

She stops to rest under an apricot tree with a few fruits left. She pulls down a drooping branch, shaking it vigorously until an apricot falls. She bends down and picks up the overripe fruit. With her long thumbnail, she stabs through the yellowish pink skin. Golden juice rushes out, racing down her thumb and wrist, cooling the pores of her skin along the way. She slides her sharp nail around the apricot and tears it apart into two messy halves. The large seed on one half stares at her.

"It's not that hard," she mumbles. "I can cut anything."

A large, black creature runs toward her and dives on her back. Little Trang falls, face down, but eases her crash with her hands. The apricot's halves crush in her palms.

"Uneducated dog! I'll teach you a lesson!" she curses.

Dumb Vita licks her ear and then quickly runs away. Little Trang pushes herself up. She pulls out her slingshot from her pocket. She takes the wet apricot seed in her hand and shoots it at Vita. But she misses badly. Vita barks and disappears behind some bushes.

Trang swallows her anger and continues down until she reaches the narrow creek curving behind the apricot orchard. She finds the blackberry shrubs but sees no one. Usually the children gather here and play hide-and-seek, or they hunt for squirrels and birds with their slingshots or fish for crawdads in the muddy creek with the raw chicken parts that they brought from home. She walks further down along the creek. Tall pines embed both sides of the creek now. Perhaps the children have hiked deep down the creek to find a perfect tree that extends its large branches from one side of the creek to the other, and the boys can climb up and tie a long rope on that branch so they can swing like monkeys from one side to the other.

After a long while, I become more and more reluctant to follow the little girl. I recognize this path, and I know what secret lies ahead. And suddenly, I feel weak, and I don't want to follow her any longer. But she's going down there no matter what, with or without me. Why can't a secret be a secret? But nothing can be a secret if it isn't discovered. Sometimes it is better to leave something unknown.

Chu Que always treated me like I was his pupil. But when I was old enough, I realized that he was only about fifteen years older than me, so I told him to cut that act out. And he did. He had to. I was a young woman now, and I could easily live on my own any day. In a way, Chu Que was relieved to be rid of the fatherly responsibility of all those years.

We became friends, friends in the way that we could swear at each other freely, and run away from each other for a few days, until we crawled back in the same corner and shared our cup again. Our difference in age didn't matter anymore. In a way, we were immortal.

"We're angels on the streets," Chu Que described us.

"But angels are the slaves of God," I contradicted him. "They are worse off than beggars."

Chu Que was very handsome. A brave soldier dressed in a new uniform couldn't be as handsome. He was neither tall nor did he carry himself well, especially with his limp. But he had the saddest face in Saigon. Every time I looked at him I felt very fortunate for my own life. His eyes, which were long and deep as the creek here, could see through any soul. Every day, we sat around and observed people on the streets. And randomly as he chose, Chu Que would point his finger at any person and tell me about him or her like he had known that person for years.

So I began to love. I don't know how or exactly when or what for, but I did, like I can't help but dream when I sleep. And everybody has to sleep, even if they live outside on the streets, and it's raining. And in Saigon, did it rain. It was late that August when the monsoon had come down hard for eight straight days and still wouldn't quit. Standing on the sidewalk, the flood had risen to our knees. That night I lost my sandals as we waded for many blocks to find a high step on some house or building. But with Chu Que's leg, we moved slowly, so all the dry spots were occupied by other beggars. We searched for miles with no luck.

"We're going to drown tonight," I said to him.

"Don't be silly. There must be a dry place somewhere in this damn city." He cried.

I could hardly hear him. The storm pounded hard against metal sheet rooftops, and water gushed down the sidewalks. The wind shoved violently, snapping tree branches and knocking over parked cyclos and scooters. Our streets became a river of floating trash. Wind and rain, earth and heaven, there must be a dry spot somewhere. We stared real hard, into the corners of brick walls, the pits of long alleys, under iron balconies and behind trash cans. And slowly, from these darkest places, round eyes, many of them, began to light up like stars, gazing out at us. We looked down with shame. We could not see our feet.

Then Chu Que said, "Follow me."

He held my hand and led me to a motel nearby. He pulled me inside the office room where the owner of the motel was leaning at the front counter. He was sipping hot tea. His wife and children were eating rice in the back.

"No," I said. "They would never—"

But Chu Que motioned me to say no more.

"How much for a room?" Chu Que asked the owner.

The owner didn't bother to answer. But his wife, she noticed how serious Chu Que seemed. So she replied, "Four hundred dong."

Chu Que slowly bent his back. He untied the knot on the short leg of his trouser. A tightly-wrapped plastic bag fell out, and Chu Que caught it. He took off the rubber band and unwrapped the plastic bag. Inside was a roll of money, a big roll of small bills. He counted the money in front of the owner and his wife.

"Here's the four hundred," Chu Que said. "And there are twenty-three left. I will throw that in also if you make us a pot of hot tea like that and give us your leftover rice."

Astonished, the owner nodded. His wife took the money.

The owner showed us our room. A short while later, the wife served us hot tea and rice with salted fish and sour cabbage.

Chu Que and I both removed our soaked clothes, and we wrapped ourselves with the blankets that the room provided. We ate our rice and drank our tea. It was our best meal together.

After that, we crawled onto the bed and laid next to each other, like we always did on the street anyway. Only this time we were naked. I asked him about the money since I was as surprised as the motel owner. Chu Que shook his head in regret. He said he had been saving it to buy me a sweater. I inched closer to him. I told him that I already had him to keep me warm. Then his hand crawled slowly beneath the blankets and found its place on my small breast and covered my cold nipple. And just like that, we discovered ourselves all over again. And after an hour or so, we held tightly to each other and rolled down to the floor because we weren't used to lying on a soft mattress. I remember we giggled like little kids.

After that night, our lives changed completely. We still begged and dragged ourselves on the streets as usual. But I mean the invisible changes that you can't see. Whatever it was, it was comforting to know that someone would always be there for me, even though he was there since the beginning.

But nothing lasts. Money has to be spent, and food has to be eaten or it will spoil. Why discover something when one cannot hold on to it forever?

The night Chu Que died, we were sitting on Le Loi Boulevard, near Ben Thanh Market. Many things had changed. For one thing, Saigon was now Ho Chi Minh City, but we beggars couldn't care less. I was only worried about Chu Que's health. He was in constant pain. At night, he couldn't sleep in peace, always tossing and turning inside our blanket, ending up crouching like a fetus that tucks its hands in front of its stomach. I held him still as much as I could with one hand, and with the other hand, I massaged his head since it helped to ease his pain a little. I took him to the hospital, but it was no use. The doctor told us that he would require surgery, and there were other poor sick people with worse cases waiting.

"What are we supposed to do?" I asked the doctor. "Just wait to die on the street?"

The doctor said nothing.

"Let's go," Chu Que told me. "It's not his fault."

That night we sat in our corner. I was too tired to beg so I leaned back against the wall. The apartment's balcony above cast a shadow over my body. Chu Que, skinny and weak, crawled out to the sidewalk to be visible under the streetlights. It was nice to see him from a distance. He was indeed a poet in the degradation of time and mass. Sitting by myself, I watched him play his last game of words.

A man with black boots walked by.

"Chu a Chu, do you know what time it is?" asked Chu Que before he looked up and saw that the man's green hat glittered with a red metal star.

"It's ten after nine." The man's metal watchband and the large buttons on his khaki uniform shined at us. "Why do you ask? Does it matter to you what time it is?"

"No. I guess not. But a long time ago, I used to have a nice watch and I always knew what time it was…and…and I used to wear leather shoes that warmed my feet…and I used to live in a large house that had a tall ceiling to shield my head from the rain…like your beautiful hat there. No. I guess I don't need to know what time it is. It's just an old habit of this…poor…bum." And then Chu Que coughed abruptly.

The tall man stared at Chu Que for a while before, finally, he pulled out a hundred dong bill and dropped it in Chu Que's bowl.

"And did you used to have two legs, too?" asked the man.

"Huh? Two legs, one leg, what's the difference, dong chi?" Chu Que acknowledged him as Comrade.

"It's obvious."

"No, it's not. I'm almost blind, so why don't you tell me the difference between two legs and one leg."

The man shook his head and was about to leave.

"Tell me, or you don't know, dong chi!"

"All right, since you want to know so bad. I walk, you skip. I run, you crawl."

"You forget that you work and I beg, you give and I take!"

"You're right." The man laughed and dropped the second hundred dong bill. As the man turned away, Chu Que suddenly coughed out in a fury.

"Let me tell you what's the difference between two legs and one leg. Listen up. There's no difference! You and I are stuck together like a kite with a tail and a head, understand? Without my tail, you can't fly straight with your big head. Without a beggar like me, you'd have no one to show off your wealth to. Without me, you're nothing!"

The man in black boots laughed even louder. He walked away in long strides.

Chu Que died that night, in defeat at his own game, leaving his Cho Con by herself in this world. Before he passed away, he gasped by my neck, "Leave this place."

I wrapped his body and crutch inside two blankets, his and mine, and tightened them with the same rope that he once used to put around my neck. I paid a cyclo to take us to the border of the Saigon River. There, I slid his body into the black water. I was hoping that his body would flow out to reach the South China Sea and then to the Pacific Ocean. But instead, Chu Que's body just sank and vanished, carrying all the weight of his pain with him.

I knew that I couldn't play the game of wit any longer. It wasn't a game anymore. It was begging now. Chu Que and I had lied to ourselves. In truth, we weren't poets. We were bums on the streets who begged for a living. We begged for meals. We begged for cigarettes. We begged for clothes. We begged for shelter. And after Chu Que died, I begged my way to America.

I took the bus from Ho Chi Minh City to Vung Tau, the peninsula where the Bay of Boats was located. In the daytime, I went to the restaurants, the villas, and the cafes that lined the resort's beach, and I begged. But at night, I walked to the Bay of Boats, and I sat and waited. I waited for weeks before one night I saw people creeping out like spiders from the darkest corners. I knew it was the moment, and I quickly changed into a clean outfit that I had saved. I crawled quietly from behind and slowly, I rose and joined them. No one noticed that I was an outsider. We waited, at least fifty of us, by the shore with our heads low, until these small boats that looked like coffins became visible in front of us. We waded out quietly and climbed on. The small boats rowed out in an hour between water and blackness. We reached a much larger fishing boat that had been waiting for us, and we crawled over quickly. The fishing boat sailed out for hours before daring to turn on its motor. The boat people crouched on deck, leaning on each other, seasick, like spiders entangled in their own web.

We reached Malaysia in seven days. No one knew I cheated. They were too happy to care. I spent seventeen months at a refugee camp before I was sponsored to America by a Catholic church in Fresno.

For many years, I worked as a custodian in an elementary school. I swept and mopped and days dried by. I sorted the papers, pencils and crayons that were dropped on the floor, and I tried to piece my life together. But most of the time, I picked up little pieces of trash and threw them in a large garbage can, and I dumped the loose fragments of my life in with them. Eventually, I had nothing left of myself to throw away.

And now I stare at the muddy water in this creek, and I wonder if this water carries any trace of Chu Que. It must. A body of water merges into other bodies of water, no matter how different they are in volume, in salt concentration, or in geography. Water from a river in one country flows out to join a sea, then meets an ocean, then travels a long distance to meet another sea, then joins a river in a new country, and ends up in a little creek. What do I know anyway? One leg or two legs, on boat or not, it still takes one to the same place. There's no difference.

I see no more need to follow little Trang. Obviously, she would never see me, and even if she could, she doesn't need my teaching. In this land, no one wants to beg, even if one is a beggar, and no one wants to play a game of wit, and definitely one would not pay for it. One just gives what one feels like, and one takes more than one can carry.

I jump into the creek and let the water carry me. It's something that I wanted to do three days ago but never had a chance. The water encloses my body, merges into me and stretches me. If I stay in this water long enough, gradually, I'll become the creek.

The water carries me, and I flow past little Trang who is still trotting anxiously further down the creek. The water takes me by many pines before it brings me back to the pathetic woman sitting by the creek with her bare feet in the water. Her back leans against a large trunk, but her head tilts toward the ground like she is about to fall down. She has one skinny hand clutching at her neck. Her eyes, pale yellow and barely open, gaze down at the water.

What are you staring at, you miserable woman? Why are you sitting there by yourself at a place like this? How did you end up here, Cho Con?

I grab her feet and pull myself out of the water. I sit next to her. I ask her many questions, but she does not respond. I wave my hand in front of her eyes, but she does not blink. I poke and tickle her feet but she does not move. At one point, I try to creep inside of her.

Damn you, you're worthless, useless, nothing but a heavy bag of rice.

Soon little Trang walks by, and she sees the woman sitting by the creek with her bare feet in the water. She stops before the woman and asks, "Aunty, have you seen any boys and girls walking by here?"

Forget it little girl. She won't answer you. She can't. She's dead.

"I've been looking for them, but I can't find them anywhere. We were supposed to meet and play down there." She points to the direction where she came from. Then she grins, showing off her little teeth. "Have you seen them, Aunty?" They're small, like me."

The woman has a black bag open on her lap. A strong breeze flies by and knocks the bag off her lap. Green bills of ones, fives, and tens roll out of the bag and hang loose at its mouth.

"Aunty, there's your money. You better put them back inside your bag, or they're going to fly into the water and get all wet."

Take the money, little girl. There are twenty-four dollars and some coins there. This woman does not need money any longer. She has begged all her life, and now she has a chance to give some back. Please take her money, little girl. Don't you want to help your mother? Take the money and give it to her. Take the spare change, little girl, and return this woman a favor.

A stronger wind rushes by. The bills flap loose, but little Trang quickly kneels down and grabs them. She puts the bills on the ground and rolls them into a tight bundle. Then she tucks the money back inside the bag. As she does this, she sees several apricots resting inside.

"My mother thinks I cannot cut apricots. I can, I know I can, if only she gives me a chance. What's so hard about cutting apricots?" asks little Trang. "There you go, Aunty. I put your money back inside your bag. Be careful now."

You old fool. You didn't think this would happen to you, right? You thought that on the anniversary of Chu Que's death, you would walk across the broad apricot orchard near where you live, pick a few apricots, and hike to the little creek here. You thought that at this creek, you could take off your shoes and cool your feet in the water. And you thought that you would have time to share a few apricots with Chu Que. You thought you would have time to do all that before you'd drown yourself so you could join him in the creek here. But what do you know? You died before you could do much. You died as you choked on an apricot's seed.

"What's in your hand? What are you hiding?" asks little Trang. "My sister plays a guessing game with me all the time. She hides a coin in one hand and makes me guess."

Little girl, would you do me a favor and push my body into the water. As long as it sits here, I cannot rest in peace. As long as it stays there, I'll never join him.

Little Trang bends down and holds up the tight left fist of the woman. She peels out one finger at a time. Resting inside the white palm is the other rotten half of the apricot, the half without the large brown seed.

Loud barking suddenly echoes through the pines. Little Trang turns around. Black Vita is charging toward her. She drops the woman's hand to pull out her slingshot. She picks up several pebbles from the ground. And quickly, she races toward Vita, head to head. She aims at its nose. The dog sees the slingshot and retreats. But little Trang chases after it.

"I'll get you this time, you dumb dog! I'll get you this time!"

Please don't go.

But little Trang has disappeared after Vita.

I lean back on the pine and stare at the profile of the dead woman. She's there and I'm not, like an apricot without the seed inside. I pity her, love her more. I think I will sleep under this tree tonight.

Sestina

Christian Langworthy

I have killed the butterflies in my stomach, and my mother sits by the kitchen counter and stares at a tub of unsalted butter. She prepares an afternoon picnic for the Fourth of July.

I imagine my father down in the cellar, tinkering with the lawnmower engine. I hear his ratchet wrench biting on the engine's boltheads. I think he will come up, as he usually did on a Saturday, to shoot at the blackbirds which drop shit on our pool. His shotgun still leans against the wicker chair on the patio. At the edge of the woods, four blackbirds candle the branches of an elm.

My mother carries a Tupperware tub of macaroni salad out to the mahogany picnic table. She does not look at the shotgun. In the hot, humid air, I hear a swarm of flies buzzing over the potato salad, the hot dogs and the pickled beets. My mother swats away the flies. I open the screen door and walk to the table. A shadow streaks across the bottom of the pool. "Gary, they're at it again," my mother mumbles as she puts seasoning on the salad. "Mom, you're putting sugar on the macaroni instead of salt. Mom!" She stops, suddenly aware of what she is doing. "I don't know where my mind is these days," she says as she looks up. "Here, we'll blend it in."

All the butterflies I have killed lie on the cement patio. White butterflies. Yellow butterflies. Green butterflies. The picnic table is set with plastic forks, knives, and spoons. A slight wind licks the corners of the tablecloth, folding the cartoon faces of several Hanna-Barbera characters. The wind picks up a bit and stirs the butterflies around my feet. I swat away more flies. My mother has already gone back into the house. I feel her gaze on the back of my neck. A gust of wind blows the butterflies onto the table. I pick them off the table and flick them down to the cement. My mother says something through the kitchen window, but I can only see her lips move.

My father is back again from his long absence. He walks around on the patio, patrolling the edges of the swimming pool. An inner tube drags its shadow across the blue pool liner. My father takes his false teeth out and sets them on the table. He starts scooping leaves out of the pool with a fishnet. "Gary!" My mother shouts. "Put those back in your mouth. You're setting a bad example for the kids!" My father laughs as he always laughed, gumming a few words as he scoops up soggy maple leaves.

I pull at my own teeth with my fingers, but they don't budge. I sit down at the table to inspect the food that has been laid out. I move the butter so that it is next to the sourdough bread. I put the salt and pepper shakers together. Next are the hot dogs and rolls. I place the potato salad at one end of the table, the macaroni on the other. The butterflies are now swirling around. One lands on the back of my hand for an instant and is blown off by the wind. My hand has a smudge of yellow powder on it.

The wind suddenly dies down, and the butterflies drop to the patio cement. The buzzing of the flies gets louder and louder. I look at the butterflies in my life—the white butterflies that flew among the rows of tomato plants in the weedy garden and flew among the clotheslines—the green butterflies bobbing erratically in the summer breeze—the yellow butterflies clinging to the windowsills. I inspect the smudge of yellow dust on my hand and go into the kitchen to wash it off, remembering an old superstition that the powder of butterflies can crack dishes and pottery. The water from the faucet is cool and washes the yellow smudge off quickly. My mother has gone back out onto the patio again.

I look out the window, past the wind chimes dangling from the top of the window, and I see flies swarming around the unsalted butter. My mother looks old. She does not say much anymore. All of her energy is spent on preparing for the picnic. The tub of butter has a deep hole in it from the huge chunk she has gouged out for the table setting. Soon, her other sons and daughters will arrive, and she will feel that her life has meaning.

My father returns. He sits in the wicker chair, cradling the shotgun as he guards the pool. Two blackbirds sit perched on the elm's branches. He gets up, shotgun in hand, and walks down the path through the rose garden. My father shoots. A branch snaps and collapses, but the blackbirds fly off unharmed.

My mother stands across from me at the counter. She looks down into the tub of unsalted butter. Sunlight filters in through the screen door and brightens the butter. It is difficult to hear anything but the buzzing of the flies around the picnic table and an occasional wind brushing against the house. The picnic table is covered with butterflies. Their wings are in the pickled beets, the unsalted butter, the hot dogs and the potato salad. Some are trapped by the strong wind against the flapping tablecloth and, when the wind dies, the flies rush back to claim the food again.

I have killed the butterflies in my stomach and my mother smiles; her teeth showing above the butter, her lips quivering for an instant as if she will say something before the flies finish off her sentences. She told me once that she could hear the butterflies, that she could hear them in the breeze in the night, in the woods along the creek. All the white, green, and yellow butterflies on the mahogany picnic table.

The table is set, and I go out and stretch in the sunlight before sitting on the bench. I swat the flies off the unsalted butter and pick butterflies off the food. The wind scatters the butterflies and tumbles them along the patio and pretty soon, the butterflies are gone.

The sun is hot on my back. My mother sits down at the picnic table, and I half expect my father to walk up the path through the rose garden, but he doesn't. The butterflies are no longer in my stomach, so I pick up the false teeth from the table and hand them to my mother, and she takes them into the house. Only when she comes back after the teeth have been put away, do we eat.

The White Horse

Nguyen Ba Trac

To a country as law-abiding and orderly as America, Mr. Nguyen is not a good citizen. When it comes to income taxes, he's a mess. He doesn't file his taxes on time. He spends everything he earns, while his salary comes to him without deductions. He is enthusiastic about sending gifts to Vietnam, but when tax filing deadlines arrive, he'll be penniless. This has gone on for three years.

To the bank, Mr. Nguyen isn't a favored customer. Like an American consumer, he keeps an account and checkbook, but does no accounting, even simple addition or subtraction. He is routinely fined for overdrawing on his account. His name is registered in books and kept in computers that can expose those with bad credit. People whose names are in these computers can't be trusted. There's no lending to such people. No mortgages for them. The banks send him polite letters apologizing for not wanting him as a customer.

To the Department of Motor Vehicles and the police, Mr. Nguyen is a careless man. In a span of three years, he has received over forty tickets for moving violations. His license has been revoked twice. In the computer, late charges on such tickets continue to multiply twice, three times the original amounts, becoming figures too large for Mr. Nguyen to deal with. The same violations keep recurring: running a red light or a stop sign. Traveling too fast or too slow on the highways.

Why is he such a mess?

To be fair, Mr. Nguyen isn't exactly someone with an antisocial attitude. He's never been indicted. He's in relatively good health. He can't really complain about his mental health. When something fun happens, he can be jovial. He knows when he's sad. Nothing extraordinary about that. If he were to feel no pain or not get burnt when he sticks his hand in a fire, well then that would be a surprise. But for a Vietnamese cast far from his family, his friends, and his homeland, mired in endless worries, remembrance, and sorrow…a mind churning with events, questions, introspection…in the final analysis, this is nothing extraordinary.

Morning: brushes his teeth, cleans his mouth. Goes to work. Eats his lunch. An evening meal. Sleeps when night comes. Runs errands on weekends: buys the odd pieces of black fabric, some tablets, waiting until he can fill up a gift box to send home to his family, parents, brothers and sisters, wife and kids. It's not a heavy schedule, but he's always busy. Why?

You can't say Mr. Nguyen lives in one place. Rather, he lives in two worlds: his soul is in America, but his spirit shuttles back and forth between America and his homeland way on the other side of the globe. One moment he's sitting beneath fluorescent lights, working among various machines, the next he's walking down a Saigon alley, beneath the shade of a fish roe tree. In addition, Mr. Nguyen lives in two time periods: the present and the past. He moves back and forth within his past. Sometimes he goes all the way back to a classroom in a Hanoi temple, reciting his ABCs alongside friends afflicted by eye and skin diseases. The next moment he speeds forward to a university dorm room, where he coolly whistles as he combs his hair, getting ready for a stroll in downtown Saigon.

Such a jumbled sense of time and space can consume his entire day.

You have to admit, the earth was once a massive thing. To travel once around the globe was quite an achievement. To travel with one's tent from Hanoi to Hue for the mandarin examination took three long months. But, things change. Airplanes and spaceships have shrunk the earth. Satellite photos from outer space reduce the earth to the size of an orange. Fascism and feudal regimes have gone out of fashion. The conflict between capitalism and communism wouldn't mean much either if the earth were attacked by aliens from Venus.

But even if modern technology has reduced distances...and no matter how fast a thought can travel...nothing can quite help Mr. Nguyen (as he sits behind the wheel daydreaming about his old neighborhood in the Ban Co District) to stop his car in time for a red light in America.

Usually, he can't make it.

So, the speed of a thought is really still too slow. And space is still too large. And Mr. Nguyen still has police cars chasing him with sirens screaming full blast and lights flashing, all because of ancient reasons: running a red light. Not stopping at a stop sign. Traveling too fast or too slow on the highways.

In America, heaven and earth are turning white.

The green mountains have changed to a silvery gray, and snow dots their summits. Darkness comes swiftly now. People are shopping and celebrating Christmas, but Mr. Nguyen hasn't stopped traveling back and forth between the past and present, between this and the other side of the globe.

The turmoil between time and space creates more complications than the damn traffic citations or bank credit.

In moments of solitude, people's memories burrow back into the deepest parts of a land on the other side of the globe where they were born, digging up the upheavals in history, a history either meticulously recorded or carelessly written, a history that people can begin to question only now.

Memory takes people back to the Highlands, the Midlands, conjuring for them the haunting calls of the Lang Son rooster, even if they've never been to Lang Son before. Such memories are ephemeral. They are like the foggy image of a boat leaving the Thua Phu bank to float up the River of Perfume on a moonlit night, going upstream toward Thien Mu Pagoda, or Quan Thanh. If you were to dip your hands into the water, you might imagine being able to grab hold of the costumes of the emperors from the Nguyen Dynasty, who once brought warriors from the West all the way back to Vietnam. Such memories allow you to imagine how you once meandered about on a summer night...to imagine you're back near the Hang Co train station, looking for that insect that is sadness, the cicada...or that time when you watched the Moroccan soldiers from the French Foreign Legion.

For Mr. Nguyen, memory and an analytical mind create such headaches. For, if memory and an analytical mind can transport him to moments of past happiness, they can also fill his heart with pain. Unfortunately, thinking about the sufferings of the past doesn't help the heart to avoid being hurt.

Memory is a horse on an ephemeral path, but you can't stop it. It goes where it wants to go. It goes all the way back to Dalat, galloping freely upon green hills in an afternoon in which the hues of sunshine are as light and thin as smoke and clouds. In such moments, all he wants is for Mrs. Nguyen to hold his hand and to go wandering with her under the sun. The horse will stretch its body to take him at great strides back to his old school. To visit his old friends. Or the graves of millions of people. To relatives North and South, people who have gone through untold seasons of separation. People in prison. People hugging their knees in reeducation camps. Men, women, children who died at sea. Bombs, land mines, traps. Russian weapons, American weapons, Japanese weapons, Czech weapons. Mongolian horses. Chinese swords and machetes dating from all dynasties.

Mr. Nguyen sits at work, his hands under his chin, ignoring the ringing telephone. He looks out the window and notices the arrival of the tenth winter. His memory forces him to examine himself and all his loved ones. Even acquaintances. All the people born where he was born during a season of floods, three years before millions of people died of famine. A country that for several millennia has not seen the end of suffering.

Memory and an analytical mind take him back to the time when the French had just arrived in Vietnam with battle ships, cannons, boots. Fortress walls falling under rockets. Vietnamese heroes calmly taking poison. His memory takes him back to Christmas seasons, when Catholics were persecuted and missionaries arrested and executed; to a time when the first Vietnamese Catholics were considered bridges for Europeans to take over and dominate Vietnam. History and politics become headaches that haunt the Vietnamese mind wherever it lives in the world.

It isn't right to have to deal with worries of a political nature during Christmas. All misunderstandings must end. Christmas must be a season of love and joy.

It is now Christmas.

Streets are decorated with lights and flowers. Miniature red and green light bulbs surround the windows. Each home has prepared a lovely pine tree, properly placed in the living room. Americans seriously welcome Christmas just like the Vietnamese abandon themselves to celebrate their Tet festival.

The weather is clear and crisp. Bells toll, sending Mr. Nguyen back twenty-five years, when girls in white lined up in church to sing "Silent Night."

Mr. Nguyen tenderly remembers his first love. The girl, whose smile was bright as an apricot blossom and sweet as an orchid, had given him some fabric on Christmas Eve so that he could have a shirt made. For a seventeen-year-old boy, it was an overwhelming feeling. The girl had included a photo of Saint Theresa in a wooden frame as part of the gift.

These days, his heart is too old. It has grown too arid to feel the romance and saintliness of twenty-five years ago.

Still, the horse in his memory gallops back to that Christmas, gingerly returning to him details, such as when he came home to tell his mother about the gifts. His mother said, "Then you must buy her a gift in return." His mother undid the safety pin from her pocket and took out three bills of five dong and handed them to him. He circled the shops on his bicycle but could not think of a gift for her. What could he buy her? He settled on a pair of red velvet sandals. They were small for his feet but were still a size and a half larger than hers.

That Christmas Eve, when the bells sang out, she wore a white ao dai tunic with the oversized sandals and toyed with a white scarf in her hands. She and other girls, also in white ao dai, stood solemnly on a wooden platform outside the church, looked upward, and sent their voices soaring into the sky above the city.

He thought then that each and every soul was lined up just as solemnly, silent as could be, listening to the song that penetrated the darkness. Listening to the gentle, joyful, echoing voices that sounded like bells from far away, swaying in the realms of ancient times.

In a holy night far away, a holy night long ago
She stood dream-like in a quiet space,
A girl in a white dress and a white scarf;
A pure soul singing poetic innocence.

The girl in a white dress and a white scarf with a pure soul wasn't really a saint. She moved with her parents to another province, and Mr. Nguyen never saw her again. But she remains a pure soul forever.

Mr. Nguyen possesses a murky understanding of the Catholic saints, except, perhaps, the saint Theresa, the one in the photo that the girl had given him in high school. His understanding of Catholicism is just as murky. Once in a while, he reads the Bible, but remembers only a romantic passage: "Witness the bird in the wild. Without planting a seed, my father has allowed it to be properly fed. Witness the lilacs in the fields. Without weaving threads, my father has allowed them to be dressed in lovely clothes that even Solomon couldn't have."

When he was a child living in Hanoi, Mr. Nguyen used to stand in front of the church, watching people selling pictures of far-away Italy. Back then, printing technology in Vietnam was still rudimentary. There were pictures of floating angels or beautiful shepherds, saints with golden halos, Gothic architecture that provoked saintly emotions. Such images today continue to bring him to church during the Christmas season.

Mr. Nguyen's memory, a white horse raising its head to travel through golden fields and green hills, returns him to the sound of ringing bells from years past. Such bells ring out every Christmas. To tell the truth, his memory should rest there. Where there is a girl in her white dress and oversized sandals. She stands with her friends, forever looking skyward to sing for a peaceful and compassionate humanity. Such songs are always beautiful. Even if you're Muslim, Buddhist, or Hindu, or even an alien from Mars visiting the earth, you would feel peaceful inside. Who does not want such peaceful moments?

And if you happen to be thinking about such peaceful moments and happen to pay no attention to the stop sign, or the red light, or your account balance, then the whole business about your bad driving records, your bad credit...well, such a business is really a lovely quality, not something to be punished for.

Translated by Nguyen Qui Duc

Untitled

lê thi diem thúy

Nothing but the negative
of my sister buried in swathes of pink cloth
in a coffin tilted upright
for a photograph to which
I have only held this negative

So her face is strangely
electric
shining bright as a coquettish moon
in the center of that hair which,
brooding blue black,
is hard to separate from the dark of the coffin

Like I say,
her face is
electric
and her body is a bundle of
pink
cloth
I don't see hands or feet
(I am the type who looks for
the twist of fingernails
and
the curve of toes
attune to peculiarities)
but there's nothing more peculiar
than the way she remains floating
as though death itself just happened to
get in the way
of some place she was heading for

This negative itself
a poor record of a place
she's already
been
to

Gone

What stays are
my fingerprints
washing over film

Big girl, Little girl

lê thi diem thúy

wearing her dress
like i wear her name

don't you know?
sweat makes it mine
it means i'm here and living
when it was yours you drenched it in
ocean
water
soaked it wet with your death
ma had to keep it in the silky compartment of her suitcase
folded small and tight like a secret
and like a secret, it never dried

...

if i hadn't dragged this dress out of the attic
it would have spilled out
and me,
the biggest girl now that you're gone
i would have had to swish you round the floor
until everything you spilled was soaked dry
by this dress
...
isn't it better
i dry it on my body
each drop of sweat
pushing back the waves so that
when i'm the age you left
dying
i will have pushed the entire ocean out
and gone leaping across it
both legs kicking in the air
the way we used to leap over jump ropes
running to meet on the other side

it didn't even touch me, we'd say

Chickens

Dao Strom

The relatives were waking up. Hus Madsen could hear them moving around inside the van and the storage shed where they had slept in their sleeping bags. The relatives had arrived just two days before, and this was their first visit to the Madsens' new home and only the second time Hus had ever met them in the five years he and Tran had been married.

Hus took his cigarettes and went down the hill to smoke and admire the view. Walking down the steep driveway, he kicked up the fresh red dirt with his boots and stepped onto the concrete foundation they had poured for the house just last week. He stood there and looked out over the valley with his arms folded across his chest. He could see the mid-August sun rising over the mountains and the river winding soundlessly through the bottom of the valley.

Behind him, from the top of the driveway, he heard the dogs' collars jingling and their paws scraping excitedly on the ground as the trailer door banged open against the sharp, clean morning air. Then, he began to hear the voices of the relatives. They spoke in slow, broken English, or rapidly and loudly in their native tongue which he didn't understand a word of. He had insisted, when he married Tran, that they speak only English in their home. It was more important for the children to speak the language of the country they were growing up in than for them to be clinging to a culture they had left. It was what he had done coming to America, twenty-two long years ago, and if they were to succeed in this society, it was what they would have to learn as well.

Of the three children, only the youngest girl was his by blood. The other two had come with their mother from Vietnam by plane, just three months before he had met them. While in the refugee camp, Tran had written an article about her and her children's experiences, which had been published in a Sacramento newspaper. At that time, it had been eighteen years since Hus had come from Denmark to America, and he had been in Sacramento looking into a transfer of air bases when he read the story. He had felt so sorry because he had heard these stories before; he knew these people could prosper if only someone could give them the chance and the right circumstances. And then it occurred to him. He had no one else. He was forty-two years old, still living alone. He had a cat, a Siamese the lady upstairs had asked him to watch when she went away on vacation, and then had never come back. He was not an unattractive man, rather the opposite. Women had often said things to him, that he looked like he should be on TV But all these women he had known were flighty and frivolous, and they got on his nerves. He had given up. These women, they knew nothing of struggle, or hardship, or endurance. They would never understand him, the things he had gone through. But here, as he read the story in the paper, here was a woman for whom life had not been easy. Here was a woman who had endured, who possessed character. He sat in his tiny two-room apartment and wrote a letter to the newspaper. He wanted to do something for this woman who was a fighter. It meant something to him. What could he do, he wrote.

When they met, his heart went out to her and to himself also, in a strange way. They were married two weeks later.

* * *

The girls were coming down the hill, holding hands with the girl cousin. He couldn't remember all the cousins' names, and he couldn't pronounce them all, either. There were seven of them and the second-oldest was the only girl, named Huong, maybe seventeen. He knew her because he thought her the most pleasant and considerate of all the cousins. When they ate dinner, the boys left their plates on the table, and Huong did all the cleaning. As they came down the hill, he called out to them, "Well, good morning! Come and look at the view. I'll bet you've never seen a view like this before." He held his cigarette away from his lips as he spoke.

His daughters, he noticed, had been dressed up in the flimsy, strapless dresses the relatives had brought as gifts. They had been wearing these foolish outfits both days since the relatives had arrived. Even on a woman with a full figure, the dresses would have looked nothing more than cheap, he thought. The seven year-old's dress was glittery and purple, and his four year-old was wearing a satiny blue one. They came tottering toward him down the steep drive in high-heeled shoes that were far too big for them and only made them look more ridiculous. He hadn't known what to say without seeming rude, so he had decided, from the beginning, not to even acknowledge the dresses.

"Hi Daddy," the girls exclaimed.

"Aunt Mary and I made the girls look very pretty," said Huong, smiling brightly. She was wearing a tiger-striped bathing suit and a floppy straw hat.

"Why don't you show your cousins how to take a bath?" Hus said to the girls.

The girls got excited at this suggestion. "We'll show you the way we take a bath in the country!"

"Good idea," said Hus.

He watched as the girls hobbled over to the rack of gallons and showed their cousin how to feel for the warmest gallons of water. The rack was made of wood and had black sandpaper nailed to it to absorb the sun's heat. They each picked up a gallon and started back up the hill. It was good, he thought, to see his four-year-old daughter lugging the heavy gallon of water as well as her older sister and cousins did. He heard his seven year-old explaining, "See, the sun heats up the water." He called after them, "Make sure you lather first!"

His wife came out of the trailer. She was a very small-boned woman, wearing cutoff jeans with cowboy boots. She was speaking Vietnamese with her sister, the one they called Aunt Mary, and the two of them were laughing. The sister's husband, who they called Uncle John, was smoking a cigarette, standing outside the trailer with his shirt unbuttoned to below his chest. His eyes were narrow, his brown skin mottled, and he had a straight, black mustache. He wore a cheap gold necklace and he was a skinny man, at least a head shorter than Hus. Hus had never understood men who wore necklaces. Uncle John saw Hus and waved his hand.

"Come, eat!" he said in his thick accent, and nodded his chin and waved his cigarette in the air.

Hus put a hand on his stomach and shook his head. "No, thank you," he said loudly. "I have to go check on the pups." He pointed to the doghouse on the hill. Then, he stepped off the foundation and dropped his cigarette, grinding it into the dirt with the heel of his boot.

Since the doghouse sat on a slope, at night sometimes the puppies rolled down the hill in their sleep and fell into the trench that had been dug for the septic system. The trench was six feet deep, and the dirt at the bottom was still fresh and moist. He walked along the length of the trench now, searching it. This was something he usually got the boy out of bed in the mornings to do. That morning, there were two puppies whining and clawing at the bottom of the trench. He felt some irritation that the boy had not been out there first thing in the morning to help the puppies. But the boy was a teenager, fourteen, and what more could one expect? He hopped down into the trench and picked each puppy up by the scruff of its neck. They kicked their legs and yelped. They were so young, they had not yet opened their eyes. As he held them up and looked at their soft faces, he imagined how, in or out of the trench, the world was still dark for them. He wondered, could they feel him helping them even when they couldn't see him? Later, when their eyes opened and they could see, would they recognize him as the man who had helped them?

He carried the two puppies back up to the doghouse where the mother dog was nursing the rest, and he carefully set them down among the others.

He heard voices and splashing as he headed back up the hill. Around the stump at the side of the trailer that the girls usually stood on when Tran bathed them, the cousins were loosely gathered, bathing, each with their own gallon of water, and the girls were instructing them, teetering on their high heels and still wearing the dresses. The cousins were in their bathing suits, the boys small and scrawny in their swim trunks. They were giggling and stomping and shaking themselves as they poured water over their heads. They looked like chickens. Hus couldn't believe these people were his relations.

He walked up the road toward them, lighting another cigarette, and he called out to them that it worked best if they poured the water slowly. "Just enough to get you wet first," he said. "Then put the gallon down, and lather up and shampoo. Then, rinse. Out here in the country, we have to conserve water." As they looked at him, he made lathering motions around his body to illustrate what he meant. They were laughing and smiling at him. They put down their gallons while they rubbed shampoo in their hair. Then, one of the boys picked up a gallon and splashed water at his brothers. They began to shriek and laugh and chase each other around. Seeing this, Hus waved his arms. "Hey, hey," he called, "we have to conserve water here. No horsing around now."

* * *

This was the plan Hus had designed for their sewage system: a large septic tank buried deep in the ground and twenty feet of pipe running the length of the trench across the hillside, attached at one end to the porthole of the septic tank and the other—when it was ready—to the sewage pipes beneath the house. For the meantime, however, Hus planned to leave one end of the pipe loose, so that it could be dragged up the hill and attached to the waste tank underneath the trailer at least once every week. The boy, wearing thick rubber gloves, would be in charge of this chore. Hus had already shown him the lever to open the trailer's sewer tank, thereby allowing the waste to flow down the long pipe, through the trench, into the septic tank.

The boy had said nothing, had just stared glumly at the coils of pipe as Hus explained all this to him. Hus had tried to make a joke of it, ruffling the boy's hair and chuckling, "You may hate it now, but one day you'll realize this was one of the most interesting experiences of your life! Hey, how many kids get a chance to man a septic tank every week anyway?" Of Tran's two children before Hus, only the boy was old enough to realize the changes they had gone through in coming from Vietnam and his mother remarrying. While Tran's daughter had accepted Hus easily, the boy was gloomy and reticent. Hus had tried to teach him things, fishing, distinguishing car brands, model airplanes. The boy had listened unenthusiastically, but in private, Hus discovered one day, the boy worked intently on the model airplanes or drawing pictures of cars. This frustrated Hus.

The large septic tank sat now at the top of the driveway, a huge, black submarine-shaped hunk of iron and aluminum. Today was the day Hus and the boy would drag the tank down the hill and maneuver it into the hole they had dug for it next to the trench. With two thick coils of braided rope, Hus and the boy fastened a harness around the body of the septic tank. The cousins were playing soccer with a deflated ball on the concrete foundation, the girls running after them barefoot in the ridiculous dresses, and Tran had set up lawn chairs in front of the trailer for Aunt Mary and Uncle John, who were lounging in the morning sun with glasses of iced tea to watch Hus and the boy. As they were finishing the harness, a black Chevrolet truck appeared at the top of the driveway, and a man got out.

"Howdy!" the man called out.

Hus couldn't recall ever having seen this man before, though he recognized the truck from passing it occasionally on the roads. The man was tall and wiry, in his thirties, dressed in jeans and cowboy boots. His muscles showed like knots through the thin fabric of his T-shirt, and his arms were covered with tattoos. His skin was sunburnt in patches high on his cheeks, and he wore an orange baseball cap. He had a thick mustache and walked with his hands dangling loosely.

Hus stopped halfway up the driveway. "Hello. What can I do for you?"

The man slowed down and stood a guarded distance from Hus. He looked at Hus and then behind him at the relatives and the girls and the boy. He hooked one thumb in his belt loop and rubbed his bristled chin with his other hand.

"Scuse me if I'm interruptin' your morning, looks like you're having some sorta party, and it sure is a beautiful morning." His eyes shifted beneath his thick eyebrows. "You see, my dog was shot last night. Now I know my dog wasn't the nicest dog, them pit bulls are damn crazy sometimes, but he was still a damn fine dog, and no one had the right to go and shoot him in the night like that." He paused, studying Hus. "Now I been investigating," the man went on, "and I'm just going around asking questions. I don't mean no harm. I know plenty of folk out here didn't like my dog. But I also got my rights, no one shoulda shot my dog. Now I'm just coming by t'ask you, mister, did you see or hear anything unusual last night roundabout 11:30 p.m. or so?"

"No, I'm afraid I did not," replied Hus. "Sorry."

"Well, mister," said the man, tipping back his hat and raising his chin, "can I ask you then, what were you and your folk up to roundabout that time last night?"

"We were asleep," said Hus. He remembered having heard from neighbors down the road about a pit bull sneaking around and killing chickens and chasing kids on bikes. Hus thought, it's probably a good thing that pit bull got shot. A dog's personality was nothing more than a reflection of the man who owned him. "I don't think I can help you anymore. Good luck, however." Hus turned his back to walk away, but the man raised his voice and called out after him.

"Well mister, I been hearin' maybe otherwise. Some other fella gave me your address, says you're the new people and he's seen your truck driving past my pit bull a number of times."

Hus' eyes swept over the relatives, who had come up the driveway and were standing, staring at him. He turned to face the man again, but the image of the relatives had stuck in his mind, and he saw himself as the man must have seen him with all his brown-skinned, slant-eyed relatives in a scattered line behind him, wearing their cheap secondhand clothing, the scrawny boys in their swim trunks and Huong in her floppy hat and tiger-striped bathing suit. He could read the man's disgust at the sight, and felt a shameful anger rise up inside himself because Hus understood that feeling of repulsion himself. Hus felt a pain in his stomach. His stomach was terrifically sensitive to stress and different foods, and he had developed an ulcer recently. Sometimes when the pain rose in his gut, it made him furious and wild at everything, regardless of his true intentions. Hunger and lack of discipline could do this to dogs, too, he thought. Especially pit bulls who were mean by nature and might turn on you at any moment.

"Now I don't mean to jump to no conclusions," the man said, "but I hear you mighta been out last night, and there ain't no one else around here I figure woulda shot a man's dog."

"As I already said, we were asleep."

"How do I know that for sure?" The man took a step forward and flung one arm in a palm-up gesture toward Hus. His other arm hung at his side, swaying with the natural motion of his body. It occurred to Hus that the man was probably an alcoholic. "You got yourself proof?"

"You can ask anyone here," said Hus, feeling heat rise behind his teeth.

"How do I know you ain't just goddamn lying?" the man said sternly. He put his hands on his hips and leaned forward. "How do I know maybe you weren't all up drinking last night and decided, hey, let's go out and look for a dog to shoot!"

Hus was certain the man must be drunk. "You're an insensible man," he said, "you're wasting my time."

"Hey!" Tran had come to stand a few feet behind Hus, and now both men looked at her, Hus turning halfway around. She was standing with her feet spread and her hands on her hips. In her broken English, she exclaimed, "I his wife! He was asleep with me last night, I know!" She was a small woman, and her eyes were beady behind her thick glasses. Looking at her standing there so defiantly, Hus felt embarrassed at the sight of her. He wished that she hadn't spoken up, but he also wished her statement could really be enough to end this situation.

The man made a hooting noise. "Oh, Mama," he chuckled.

He laughed again and shook his mustached face like he was impressed. He looked directly at Tran, and her face began to turn red. She took a step backwards and her gaze shifted. Her mouth opened and closed. The man shrugged, "I ain't said nothing."

Hus saw no worth in the man at that moment.

"What did I just tell you!" Hus shouted. As he strode forward, in the back of his mind he was vaguely aware of the fact that he had not just told the man anything to justify him shouting out this question. The man stumbled backwards a step, and Hus stopped a foot from him. "Get off my property," Hus said lowly. "I swear to you, you don't know what you're dealing with if you don't get off this property this instant. By God, I swear to you, I mean it." The blood had drained from his face, and he felt cold and somehow violated. He didn't want the girls to see him like this.

The man tugged on the bill of his hat and twitched his mustache. He seemed to be looking for a foothold but wasn't able to find one. Finally, he turned his back with an abrupt, jerking motion and sauntered back to his truck. Angrily, he climbed into the cab and turned over the ignition. The truck roared. There was a hissing noise in its grill. The man put his tattooed forearm on the window frame, leaned his head out and shouted, "Now listen, I won't forget this, y'hear me?" Then, he put his truck in gear and backed out of the driveway. The tires spit pebbles up out of the gravel.

Hus turned and walked stiffly back to the septic tank. His wife and the relatives and the children were all looking at him. The boy was standing close to the septic tank, kicking at it with the toe of his sneaker. His wife was still standing with her hands on her hips, her face flushed red. This is how they had all stood, Hus thought, all of them looking to him.

"That not a very friendly man," said Aunt Mary, who was standing up now in front of her lawn chair. She looked with concern toward Tran.

Hus spoke up, "She's all right now. She just has to learn that not everybody is friendly." He caught his wife's glance and could see that she was upset with him. He couldn't tell if it was because of what he had just said or if she was just upset about the whole incident. What else should he have done? He told himself irritably that she did not understand. The men in her culture were different than men in America and men where he had come from as well, and she just didn't understand that. Would she ever understand? Aunt Mary was saying something in Vietnamese to his wife. His wife said something back in a curt voice. He tried to chuckle. "Tell them that's not how everyone out here in the country is," he said, realizing that this would be the story the relatives would tell when they went back to San Diego. They would say to the people they knew, this is what people in the country are like.

He wished he could prove to them how wrong they would be.

The man returned about an hour later. He was carrying a bottle of wine in his right hand. Hus and the boy had dragged the septic tank to the edge of the driveway, and were beginning to ease it down the slope. The relatives were gathered around watching, and Hus felt he was educating them by allowing them the chance to watch this work being done. His girls sat above them all in a tree with their Barbie dolls. The chickens were pecking and scratching in the chicken coop atop the hill. The dogs began to bark when they spotted the man coming down the driveway.

The man raised his arms over his head as he approached. "I came to apologize, is all," he said, and held the bottle of wine out to Hus. "I was jumping the gun and I just wanted to come say how sorry I am for making a mess of your morning like I did."

Hus looked at the wine bottle without knowing what to do with it. He was reminded of his ulcer, which was the reason he no longer drank alcohol.

"That's fine," said Hus. It wasn't easy for him to say. He didn't want to accept the wine at all. "Tran," he called to his wife, "why don't you come take this?"

Tran came over from the trailer and took the bottle, smiling politely. Hus told himself, she'll have to learn, she shouldn't smile so sweetly at a man like this one.

The man wiped his hands on his jeans. "My name's William, by the way." He stuck out his hand, and Hus shook it. The man's hand was thin and sticky.

"Hus Madsen," he said. "My wife, Tran."

"Hello missus." The man tipped his hat. "I do apologize for my rotten behavior this morning."

Tran nodded and smiled, and carried the wine back to the trailer. The man licked his lips. "Y'know, I went down to that bastard Wes Walker's place," he said. "I was jumping the gun earlier, I realize now, because that Walker could've shot my dog, too." The boy, behind Hus, dropped his end of the rope and knelt to pet the big black mother dog, who had come up to them, tail wagging. Hus wiped his brow and propped one hand on the side of the septic tank. He wanted the man to leave so they could get back to work. "Now what do you say," the man continued, "we go on down to Wes Walker's place, and we pay him a visit? You and your boy, or even just you and me, Hoss. You're a big fella."

"I'm afraid not," Hus said, not bothering to correct the man's pronunciation.

"You know," the man interrupted, his upper body swaying, "when I came by and I told Walker my predicament, y'know what he says? He says he don't give a flying shit about my dog. And that kinda attitude, well I don't trust that." The man leaned forward, eager to convince Hus. "I told him, 'Well I don't give a shit about yer wife.' He says to me get off his property or else he's gonna shoot *me*. And I knew right there, I thought of you, Hoss, so sensible and calm, ain't it apparent, I tell myself, that man there was an intelligent man—and it was plain to me then that Wes Walker must be the man who gone out last night and shot my dog." He grinned assuredly. "Now what do you say, huh? I just want some company along."

Hus frowned. "We're too busy here to help you with that."

The man removed his hat and spun it on his fingers. He wiped at his flattened hair. "Wouldn't take more than a minute. We go there, we show 'im, we leave."

"Dad," said the boy, hesitantly, "I still wanna go swimming today."

"You be quiet now," Hus told the boy, who immediately looked down at the dirt and stopped petting the dog.

Hus turned back to the man. "We have work to do here," he said. "I can't help you. It's none of my business. I'm sorry about your dog."

"Well, I understand," said the man, and put his hat back on. "Enjoy the wine." He left them without saying good-bye.

Hus and the boy had gotten the septic tank down the hill and were maneuvering it into position above the hole. They had to brace themselves against the weight of the tank, Hus in front pulling the rope over his shoulder and leaning so far forward his knees almost dug into the ground, and the boy at the back of the tank, pushing. Slightly irritated by the heat and work, Hus found himself wondering if the boy was pushing as hard as he could. The girls had climbed down from the tree and were running around, chasing the chickens out of the way of the oncoming tank, waving their Barbie dolls in front of them. Hus was afraid they might fall into the hole or the trench, and they were distracting him. "Get out of the way!" he was shouting at them, when he heard the man's truck again.

The man strode to the edge of the driveway and stood with his feet spread and his fists on his hips. "Hey!" he called down. "I gotta talk to you, Hoss."

Hus wiped his brow and let go of the rope. He walked to the end of the tank and stopped beside the boy. The boy shielded his eyes and looked up the hill at the man. Hus folded his arms across his chest. The two of them were sweating and dusty.

"What's the problem?" Hus called back to the man.

"I got a problem with my here dog that got shot last night," yelled the man.

"I thought we discussed this already," said Hus.

"I gotta say, Hoss, I think you been lyin' to me."

Hus took a deep breath and hooked his hands tiredly on his hips. He looked for a moment at his dirty shoes.

"Yeah, I think you been lyin' to me," the man repeated. "Wes Walker ain't the one who done it, and I know that cause he proved it to me. And I got some news for you—"

"You get off my goddamn property now," Hus raised his voice.

The man paced a few steps back and forth at the edge of the driveway. "No, I'm not done here. I know who shot my dog, lemme tell you—"

"No one here shot your dog," said Hus as calmly as he could.

"Yeah?" The man nodded his chin in the direction of the trailer, where Uncle John was standing. "I know something you oughta know about. I know that maybe your boy told Jungle Jose over there to sneak out in the middle of the night to shoot my dog. What about that?"

Hus stared incredulously at the man. He also saw his wife on the doorstep of the trailer, a distance behind the man. She was looking at the man's back. She had poured herself a glass of wine and was holding it with both hands. The boy shuffled his feet miserably. Hus wondered suddenly, how had he gotten himself into this situation, into this life?

"If you don't get off my property, I'm going to have to call the police," Hus threatened. But he was tired and slightly bewildered.

"Oh no! I'm not leaving yet, y'hear me?" yelled the man. "I'm not leaving until you tell me yes, my people shot your poor dog, and then you give me some money so I can go out and buy myself a new one. Another damn pit bull, that's right." The man paced back and forth, and then strode back to his truck, reached into the bed of it, and came out grunting and dragging something. He heaved it over his shoulder, carried it onto the driveway and threw it down on the rocks. The pit bull's body was limp and pale, and the bullet wound was visible in the middle of its rib cage.

Hus could not believe this. He stared at the man, furious.

The man pointed to the dead dog. "Now, listen. I'm going to leave this here for you, all right? It's all yours now."

Hus was on the driveway suddenly. He didn't know how he had gotten there. He shoved the man aside and reached for the dog. He lifted the cold body, felt the weight of it and the coarseness of its short fur against his forearms and chest, and he began to walk with it in his arms up the driveway.

The man shouted "Hey!" behind him.

They all watched him. He continued to walk, not knowing himself what he would do, down the road.

As he walked, it occurred to him what he was at that moment: a forty-six-year-old man carrying a dead dog down a dirt road. He thought about how hard he had worked in his life and the difficult choices he had made. Years ago he had left his home and never returned. He had left behind the part of himself too painful and too valuable to bear. But who that mattered understood this now? And this man here, this lazy, worthless man who had thrown his dead dog on the ground, this man would never be capable of understanding such things. This man was a worthless, filthy person who had allowed his dog to be shot. As he continued to walk, it slowly dawned on Hus that the man had probably shot his dog himself. Drunk and mad at the dog for harassing the neighbors, the man had gone out and shot his own dog. And then he had looked at the clock. He had remembered that it was 11:30 p.m. By morning, the man had convinced himself that someone else must've come out and shot the dog. This was what Hus believed, the more he thought about it, the farther he walked with the dog in his arms. Hus was sure of it.

The man yelled after him, "You lousy son of a bitch! Where do you think you're taking my goddamn dog!"

Hus stopped in the middle of the dusty road. He looked around himself at the trees and the brilliant blue sky and the sunshine. He gently let the dog's body down in the grass on the side of the road. He turned around slowly, his gaze sweeping over the tangled oak trees and pines descending into thickening clusters down the hill on one side of him. He saw his family and the relatives and his boy all scattered up the road watching him, the man pushing through them and swinging his arms. On the other side of the road, there was a driveway which Hus knew led up to the Nerwinskis' house. In the pastures alongside the driveway, there were sheep grazing.

The man caught up to Hus and stepped over the dead dog in the grass without glancing at it.

"You bastard fucker," said the man. He slammed his fist into his palm, coming toward Hus and stopping just short of touching him. "What do you think you're doing?"

"I think it's time for you to remove your dog and yourself from here. I think you've outstayed your welcome by now, don't you?"

Hus's family and the relatives were trickling down the road toward them. The boy and two of the cousins came and stood a few feet behind the man, glancing from Hus and the man to the dead dog. Hus saw his girls and Huong holding hands at the back of the crowd. His girls were carrying along their Barbie dolls.

"I've got something to say to you, Hoss," the man spoke quickly. "I know things, maybe you wouldn't be so sure of your people's innocence if you knew. I seen your boy out on his motorbike going past my place before. And I been told that just last week there was a boy on a motorbike chasing around my dog with his BB gun. I been told that just today when I was out asking questions of my good neighbors."

Hus ignored this because he believed the man must be lying. "To be honest with you," said Hus, "it's probably best your dog was shot. It was probably a mistreated animal and vicious because of your mistreatment." Hus caught sight of the boy, who was staring open-mouthed at the man. Hus felt the pain in his stomach flare all the way to his ribs suddenly. He straightened his back and tried to stand taller.

He faced the boy. "Is this true?" he asked him.

The boy began to stare at his feet. The man laughed once. "The dog was chasing me," the boy mumbled, "but it was a long time ago. I was on my motorcycle one day and I fell off because he was chasing me and he almost bit me."

Hus was mad at everyone now. "And then you fired at this animal with your BB gun, did you?"

The boy shrugged, not looking up, and shifted his feet in the grass.

"Like the time with the rattlesnake?" Hus felt himself growing sick. Maybe, he thought, it was best in life to just suspect everyone of having done something wrong. One day earlier that summer, there had been a rattlesnake under the old ping-pong table behind the trailer, and the boy had stupidly tried to shoot it with his air rifle, with his sisters standing nearby. Hus had come running and shouted at him when he saw this happening, what if a pellet ricocheted off the leg of the table and hit one of his sisters in the eye? What then?

The boy was still looking at his feet. "I didn't hurt his dog. He made me fall off my bike. And it happened a long time ago."

The man stood between Hus and the boy, looking back and forth from one to the other. The man folded his arms and grinned. Hus trusted no one, none of them.

"So you came back home and you got your BB gun and you went back out in search of that dog," said Hus to the boy. "You were so angry at a stupid dog, you went out again specifically to shoot at him. That is what they call premeditated, do you understand? How do we know you didn't decide to do this again, last night? I can't be sure of anything now, can I?"

"No, you can't," the man agreed.

The boy began to cry. This made Hus pull back and there was silence for a moment, just the boy sniffling, but Hus could only say, "You're too old to be making a scene of this." He wanted to be close to his family, but he could not bring himself to look any of them in the eye.

The man began to point his finger. "Now I'm holding you responsible, Hoss. Maybe I don't know the details, but you got something amiss here, buddy—"

Hus's wife came forward while the man was talking and put her arm around the boy. She glared at Hus, and Hus believed they were all, the relatives and kids, glaring at him in the same hateful manner. Hus felt terribly alone. The man was still talking at Hus when Tran said, "You being too hard on Ty. I think you being unreasonable. We go home now, forget everything." She nudged Ty's shoulders, trying to turn him away with her. Ty shrugged her off but followed when she started to walk away.

Hus watched them. The man's talking faltered, and he looked over his shoulder, following Hus's gaze. Tran was headed back up the dirt road toward home, and Aunt Mary and two of the boy cousins were starting to follow. Uncle John and the other boys were still looking toward Hus and the man. Hus noticed his youngest daughter was crying, and Huong knelt beside her. The older little girl was glancing rapidly between Hus and Tran, and Hus saw the little girl's dark hair swinging in a light way against her neck. It looked cheerful and nonchalant. Hus saw the dead dog in the grass and felt a wave of sadness at its plainness. It could have been sleeping.

"You take your poor dog and leave," Hus told the man. He nodded toward the driveway across the road. "I'm going to go call the police now. You can decide what you're going to do next."

Hus stepped over the dead dog and walked slowly across the road. The man didn't stop him. Hus walked up the Nerwinskis' driveway to their house. The sheep grazing in the pastures raised their heads briefly as Hus went by. Hus stepped onto the Nerwinskis' porch and rang the doorbell. The Nerwinskis were an old retired couple. They let him in, nodding pleasantly. The TV murmured in the living room, and Hus could hear the tinkling of wind chimes from outside an open window.

Hus was still sweaty and dusty, and his clothes smelled bad, he was sure.

"There's a man harassing my family," was all he could say. "I need to call the police."

The old couple directed him to the phone, and he strode across their floor, tracking clumps of dirt with his boots.

As he lay his hand on the phone, he caught sight of the dirt he had tracked over their clean floor. His stomach turned over painfully, and he abruptly moved his hand to it, frowning. The old couple's faces lit up in alarm. Then, Mr. Nerwinski brought Hus a chair. Hus sat down, leaning back and breathing heavily. Hus was unable to thank them or apologize right away. Mr. Nerwinski went back to stand beside his wife. Hus saw them, the old couple, standing in the middle of their living room watching him with wondering, sad eyes. He saw them amongst their weathered furniture and full bookshelves and the framed pictures on the walls, and a strange melancholy washed over him. He sat in their chair beside their phone on its polished oak stand until the roll of pain in his stomach subsided.

"It's nothing," Hus said then, "I'm very sorry. I'll be just a minute." He tried to chuckle to ease the awkwardness.

Mrs. Nerwinski smiled tenderly and shook her head. "Poor young man," she said.

Hus raised his chin. "No, no, I'm fine," he said and nodded briskly. He sat with his back straight and reached for the phone again. He lay his other hand on his thigh, and tried to keep his face from clouding, but he felt weak.

The man and the dog and all of Hus's family were gone when Hus came down the Nerwinskis' driveway. Hus walked back up the road home by himself. He felt hollow inside, but there was peace in the long grass that grew alongside the road and the sound of the birds in the trees.

When Hus reached the top of his driveway, he saw the trailer and Tran and the others standing about. They stopped talking when they saw him. His daughters ran up to him, exclaiming "Daddy's back!" and he patted their heads and said, "Yep, we're all home now." He picked up his youngest daughter and carried her on his hip down the driveway. When he reached the trailer, he set her down and nodded briefly toward Tran, and went inside. He poured water from the gallon by the sink over his hands. He rubbed his hands together and then wiped them dry on his jeans. He saw the bottle of wine sitting on the counter and thought that they should probably throw it out.

Hus went back outside and saw Tran and the relatives and Ty and the girls all looking toward him, all of them gathered around the front of the trailer. Their eyes gazed at him dark and blank, except for the girls, who were bumping hips in the dirt and paying more attention to the way the fabric of their dresses flared around their legs. The boy's eyes were the darkest, Hus thought.

"Everything's all right now," Hus said, and gave a reassuring chuckle. The quiet of the countryside filled his ears. He wondered if they cared what he thought or not. He pictured the boy sneaking out after the man's pit bull with his BB gun and never even mentioning it to Hus, his own father now, and Hus felt strangely hurt by this. "He won't be coming back, that man," he said. Then he added, addressing the girls, "It's time to feed the animals now. There's no reason to forget that." The girls ran to get the dog dishes, and he added, "Make sure you give them fresh water now too."

Hus looked at his wife. She was putting on the galoshes she used to walk in the chicken coop. She didn't like to walk on the chicken droppings in her good boots. Hus waved at her. The relatives had begun to talk amongst themselves in Vietnamese.

"No, no," said Hus, making a face to say it was no problem, "I'll do it. I'll feed the chickens today."

Outside the coop, Hus scooped up a cup of poultry feed and entered the chicken pen. As he scattered the feed around his feet in handfuls, the chickens surrounded him, scratching and clambering heedlessly over each other and the tops of his boots. He watched them closely and stayed still for fear of stepping on them.

from **When You're Old Enough**
Maura Donohue

Preset: Slide #1—B/W of Dad, Mom and baby
Downstage right stands a coat rack with an ao dai (Vietnamese dress), ballet cos-
tume (skirt, slippers, yellow scarves, hair barrette) and rosary beads on it. A tin
can sits on the floor. Off stage left center sits a folding chair. Downstage left lie
Simpson dolls, banana.

Light cue #1—Stage goes to black, Maura enters upstage left

HAI (FIRSTBORN)

Sound #1 goes first—Uzume Taiko (3 minutes)
Light cue #2—Slow fade up (10 count) SL side light and down light (column of
light)
Light cue #3—Add SR slides and rest of down/back light (fill stage) when dancer
begins crawling. Maura dances till music ends. Sound: stop tape when music
ends.
Light cue #4—Front light in when Maura moves mannequin

You can't say that we ever lied
We simply knew certain things needed to be kept quiet
When you're old enough to understand then we will tell you
Besides what would you have done if we had told you
We couldn't have you running down the street—telling all the neighbors
You don't understand what it was like back then
The war was still going on—even after they said it was over
We weren't forgetting
It was for your own good
When you're old enough to understand then we will tell you

Sound #2 goes—Ly Tieu Khuc (3 minutes)
Slide #2—Anh standing on lawn

I wish I'd never told you
Why are you so angry
I'm calling to ask you not to tell anyone
When they are old enough to understand then I will tell them
Can't you see how much it hurts me to have to remember this
This happened to me
It doesn't change who you are

Maura loses balance, rolls, slowly stands, begins putting hair in ponytail and walking clockwise, breaks into a skip ....
Light cue #5—Bright, cheery, warm, define a different space
Slide #3—3 Amerasian Children (Maura, Maeve, Bernard) in Girl & Boy Scout uniforms

...

FAMILY

Light Cue #6—Bring back front light (5 count)
Slide #4—Vietnamese grandmother holding baby
(Sweetly as she walks down center) Oh, you're so ugly....Yes. You're an ugly ugly baby. You've got a big nose and funny eyes. Yes. You do. Look at her, isn't she an ugly baby? Oh, oh, be careful. You see you have to watch out for the knives I've wrapped in her blanket. They're sharp. Aren't they, ugly baby?...No, no, no, sir, your daughter no cute. She very very ugly. No, sir, we not want spirits think she some great prize. Might try to steal her. Right, big nose?

Light Cue #6.1—Isolate down left
Slide #5—Dad holding baby
(Sits in chair down left, holds baby in one arm) My beautiful beautiful baby. Your Grandma can push on your nose all she wants, it's not going to change a

thing...my little Maura Catherine. Wait till Ma sees this, her first grandchild. I think we'll ask your Aunt Mary to be your godmother. What do you think about that? I bet she'll be pleased...*(to audience).* You know what we used to call her? We called her the rocket ship. No sooner would we tuck the mosquito netting under her crib then boom! The crib would start shaking and her engine would start going—bllbp, bllbp, blllllpplppppbbpppp. Oh, what a stink.

Slide #6—American aunt holding baby
Light cue #6.2—Isolate right center
(Moves chair to stage right, sits) I rememba when Brian came home from the wahr.

Slide #7—Dad receiving medal
He was so handsome in his uniform, and skinny too.

Slide #8—Parents' wedding picture
He'd brought his new wife and theya baby daaughta. She was so...cute. Like a little china dawll. She was so smawll.

Slide #9—Mom holding baby
She hardly looked big enough to have a baby herself. But we were happy to see that she was Catholic. And the baby she was holding was my Gawdchild. And they'd given her a good Christian name. Thank Gawd it wasn't one of those...Oriental ones. We never would have been able to pronounce one of those.
(Stands, makes scarf into baby, walk to center)
Light cue #6.3—Isolate down center

My name Nguyen Thi Ngoc. (Slower) Nguyen Thi Ngoc.
(Slower) Nguyen...Thi...N—G—U
Yes, N—G—U.
(Annoyed) Nguyen Thi Ngoc. Ngoc...
Nguyen...
(Gives up) My name Mai.
(Puts scarf back around neck, sits)
Light cue #6.4—Back to #6.2

Mai. Mai Donohue. That's easy enough to pronounce. (Confidentially to audience) Still sounds kinda chinky, though. Oh, now now. Love thy neighbor. She is a part of the family now.

Slide #10—Baby under Christmas tree

Oh! This is a picture of Maura's first Christmas. I put a bow on her head and sat her under the Christmas tree like a little...*(switch to narrator and stand)*

Light cue #6.5—open the space when Maura stands

...present. And right after I took the picture, she fell over....Every Christmas. Every Easter. Every Thanksgiving. Every birthday. Every First Communion (and there have been a lot). Every Holy Confirmation (and there have been a lot). Every family gathering that they could conjure up (and there have been a lot), she would tell this same story to the same group of people over and over again...to this very day. (Moves chair to center, sits)

CATHOLIC

So I grew up Catholic.

Slide #11—Maura in First Communion dress in church

(Falls off chair to knees—continues genuflecting through text—rising, crossing self and falling) And I was educated as to the inferiority *(drop)* of those heathens *(drop)* who did not believe in Our Lord, *(sit)* The Jesus Christ. I was told of their wrongness *(drop)* and of the eternal agony *(drop)* that they would suffer (drop) as a result of their failure to believe in, or indeed, *(sit)* even know about our Saviour. Phew! Boy was I glad my mom had switched to Catholicism. Just think of all my other Vietnamese relatives who are going to rot in hell forever and ever. Amen. *(Picks up rosary beads, begins chanting Hail Mary)*

Sound #3 goes—Hail Mary in Vietnamese (3 minutes)

Light cue #7—Bring down Side light—moody

Dances with rosary beads, spinning in place and then ritualistically places them in a circle

Sound #3 continues into Sableyalo Mi Agonize (4.5 minutes)
Slide #12—Genesis 3:16
Light cue #8—Isolate center down light and sides only
(Kneels, dances trying to stand, when begins putting rosary beads on, then bring up)

Slide #13—Hail Holy Queen Prayer

When music ends, slide #14—black
Light cue #9—Opens the space/cover entire stage when music ends

CHANGE

I became old enough to understand
Slide #15—Do As I Say Not As I Do

(Takes down hair, takes off rosary beads)
Sound #4 goes—Dang Dan, Mau Dao, Doc Canh

She said, "It doesn't change who you are"

It doesn't change who you are?
Who are you?

#16a—Marriage certificate (10 seconds)
#17a—Birth certificate (10 seconds)
#16b—Close-up of date (10 seconds)
#17b—Close-up of date (10 seconds)
#16c—Date (10 seconds)
#17c—Date (10 seconds)

#18—Honor Thy Mother and Father (30 seconds)

#19—Marriage (10 seconds)

*#20—**Duty** (10 seconds)*
(stops dancing, music shifts to chanting)
*#21—**Firstborn** (15 seconds)*
(begins putting on ao dai)

*#22—**Son** (10 seconds)*
*#23—**Full** (5 seconds)*
*#24—**Blooded** (5 seconds)*
*#25—**Half** (5 seconds)*
*#26—**Brother** (5 seconds)*

*#27—**First born** (10 seconds)*
*#28—**Son** (5 seconds)*
*#29—**Big Sister** (5 seconds)*
*#30—**Little Sister** (5 seconds)*
*#31—**Half** (5 seconds)*
*#32—**White** (5 seconds)*
*#33—**Yellow** (5 seconds)*
*#34—**Half** (5 seconds)*
*#35—**Child** (5 seconds)*
*#36—**Woman** (5 seconds)*
*#37—**Vietnamese** (wait till Maura faces audience)*
*#38—**American***

Light cue #10—*Blackout/last slide stays up*

END

Show and Tell

Andrew Lam

Mr. K. brought in the new kid near the end of the semester during what he called oral presentations and everybody else called eighth grade Show and Tell. This is Cao Long Nguyen, he said, and he's from Vietnam and immediately mean old Billy said cool!

What's so cool about that? asked Kevin who sat behind him and Billy said, Idiot, don't you know anything, that's where my Daddy came back from with this big old scar on his chest and a bunch of grossed out stories. And that's where they have helicopters and guns and VCs and all this crazy shit. Billy would have gone on and on but Mr. K. said, Billy, be quiet.

Mr. K. stood behind the new kid and drummed his fingers on the kid's skinny shoulders like they were little wings flapping. He tried to be nice to the new kid, I could tell, but the kid looked nervous anyway. The new kid stood like he was waiting to be thrown into the ocean the way was hugging his green backpack in front of him like a life saver.

Cao Long Nguyen is a Vietnamese refugee, Mr. K. said and he turned around and wrote "Cao Long Nguyen—Refugee" in blue on the blackboard. Cao doesn't speak any English yet but he'll learn soon enough so let's welcome him, shall we, and we did. We all applauded but mean old Billy decided to boo him just for the hell of it and Kevin and a few others started to laugh and the new kid blushed like a little girl. When we were done applauding and booing Mr. K. gave him a seat in front of me and he sat down without saying hello to anybody, not even to me, his neighbor, and I had gone out of my way to flash my cutest smile to no effect. But right away I started to smell this nice smell from him. It reminded me of eucalyptus or something. I was going to ask him what it was but the new kid took out his Hello Kitty notebook and began to draw in it like he'd been doing it forever, drawing and drawing even when Show and Tell already started and it was, I'm sorry to say, my turn.

Tell you the truth, I didn't want it to be my turn. I can be funny and all but I hated being in front of the class as much as I hated anything. But what can you do? You go up when it's your turn, that's what. So when Mr. K. called my name I brought my family-tree chart and taped it on the blackboard under where Mr. K. wrote "Cao Long Nguyen—Refugee" but before I even started Billy said Bobby's so poor he only got half a tree and everybody laughed.

I wanted to say something back real bad right then and there. But as usual I held my tongue on the account that I was a little afraid of Billy. OK, I lie, more than a little afraid. But if I weren't so fearful of that big dumb ox I could have said a bunch of things like Well at least I have half a tree. Some people they only have sorry ass war mongers with big old scars for a Daddy or I could have said what's wrong with half a tree. It's much better than having a quarter of a brain or something like that.

Anyway, not everybody laughed at Billy's butt swipe of a comment. Mr. K., for instance, he didn't laugh. He looked sad, in fact, shaking his head like he was giving up on Billy and saying, Shh Billy, how many times do I have to tell you to be quiet in my class? And the new kid he didn't laugh neither. He just stared at my tree like he knew what it was but I doubt it 'cause it didn't even look like a tree. Then when he saw me looking at him he blushed and pretended like he was busy drawing but I knew he wasn't. He was curious about my drawing, my half a tree.

If you want to know the awful truth it's only half a tree 'cause my Mama wouldn't tell me about the other half. Your Daddy was a jackass, she said, and so is his entire family and clan. That's all she said about him. But Mama, I said, it's for my Oral Presentation project and it's important but she said so what.

So nothing, that's what. So my Daddy hangs alone on this little branch on the left side. He left when I was four so I don't remember him very well. All I remember is him being real big and handsome. I remember him hugging and kissing and reading me a bedtime story once or twice and then he was gone. Only my sister Charlene remembers him well on account that she's three years older than me. Charlene remembers us having a nice house when my Daddy was still around and Mama didn't have to work. Then she remembers a lot of fighting and yelling and flying dishes and broken vases and stuff like that. One night when the battle between Mama and Daddy got so bad Charlene said she found me hiding in the closet under a bunch of Mama's clothes with my eyes closed and my hands over my ears saying Stop, please, Stop, please, Stop like I was singing or chanting or something. Charlene remembers us moving to California; not long after that Daddy left us. I don't remember any of that stuff. It just feels like my entire life is spent living in a crummy apartment at the edge of the city and that Mama had been working at Max's Diner forever, and that she smoked and drank and cussed too goddamn much and she was always saying we should move somewhere else soon, go back to the South maybe, to New Orleans where we came from, but then we never did.

So what did I do? I started out with a big lie. I had rehearsed the whole night for it. I said my Daddy's dead. Dead from a car accident a long long time ago. I said he was an orphan so that's why there's only half a tree—(so fuck you, Billy). Then I started on the other half. I know the other half real well 'cause all of Mama's relatives are crazy or suicidal and naturally I loved their stories. So I flew through them. There was my great-great-Granddaddy Charles Boyle the third who was this rich man in New Orleans and who had ten children and a big old plantation during the Civil War. Too bad he supported the losing side 'cause he lost everything and killed himself after the war ended. Then there was my Granddaddy Jonathan Quentin who became a millionaire from owning a gold mine in Mexico and then he lost it all on alcohol and gambling and then he killed himself. And there was my Grandma Mary who was a sweetheart and who had three children and who killed herself before the bone cancer got to her and there were a bunch of cousins who went north and east and west and became pilots and doctors and lawyers and maybe some of them killed themselves too and I wouldn't be a bit surprised 'cause my Mama said it's kinda like a family curse or something. I went on like that for some time, going through a dozen or so people before I got to the best part: See here, that's my great-aunt Jenny Ann Quentin, I said, all alone on this little branch 'cause she's an old maid. She's still alive too, I said, ninety-seven years old and with only half a mind and she lives in this broken-down mansion outside of New Orleans and she wears old tattered clothes and talks to ghosts and curses them Yankees for winning the war. I saw her once when I was young, I told my captive audience. Great-aunt Jenny scared the heck out of me 'cause she had an old shotgun and everything and she didn't pay her electric bills so her big old house was always dark and scary and haunted. You stay overnight and they'll pull your legs or rearrange your furniture. In summary, had we won the war a hundred years ago, we might have all stayed around in the South. But as it is, my family tree has its leaves fallen all over the States. So that's it, there, now I'm done, thank you.

Tommy went after me. He told about stamp collecting and he brought three albums full of pretty stamps, stamps a hundred years old and stamps as far as the Vatican and Sri Lanka. He told how hard it was for him to have a complete collection of Pope John Paul the Second. Then it was Cindy's turn. She talked about embroidery and she brought with her two favorite pillowcases with pictures of playing pandas and dolphins that she embroidered herself. She even showed us how she stitches, what each stitch is called and how rewarding it was to get the whole thing together. And Kevin talked about building a tree house with his Daddy and how fun it was. He even showed us the blueprint which he and his Daddy designed together and photos of himself hanging out on the tree house, waving and swinging from a rope like a monkey with his friends and it looked like a great place to hide too if you're pissed off at your Mama or something and then the bell rang.

Robert, Mr. K. said, I wonder if you'd be so kind as to take care of our new student and show him the cafeteria. Why me, I said and made a face like when I had to take the garbage out at home when it wasn't even my turn but Mr. K. said why not you, Robert, you're a nice one.

Oh no I'm not, I said.

Oh yes you are, he said, and wiggled his bushy eye brows up and down like Groucho.

Oh no I'm not.

Oh yes you are.

OK, I said, but just today. OK, though I kinda wanted to talk to the new kid anyway, and Mr. K. said, thank you, Robert Quentin Mitchell. He called the new kid over and put one arm around his shoulders and another around mine. Then he said Robert, this is Cao, Cao, this is Robert. Robert will take care of you. You both can bring your lunch back here and eat if you want. We're having a speed tournament today and there's a new X-Men comic book for the winner.

All right! I said. You're privileged if you get to eat lunch in Mr. K.'s room.

Mr. K. has all these games he keeps in the cabinet and at lunch-time it's sort of a club and everything. You can eat there if a) you're a straight-A student, b) if Mr. K. likes and invites you which is not often, or c) if you know for sure you're gonna get jumped that day if you play outside and you beg Mr. K. really really hard to let you stay. I'm somewhere in between the b) and c) category. If you're a bad egg like Billy, who is single-handedly responsible for my c) situation, you ain't never ever gonna get to eat there and play games, that's for sure.

So, Kal Nguyen—Refugee, I said, let's go grab lunch then we'll come back here for the speed tournament, what d' you say? But the new kid said nothing. He just stared at me and blinked like I'm some kinda strange animal that he ain't never seen before or something. Com'n, I said and waved him toward me, com'n, follow me, the line's getting longer by the sec', and so finally he did.

We stood in line with nothing to do so I asked him, hey, Kal, where'd you get them funny shoes?

No undostand, he said and smiled, *no sspeak engliss.*

Shoes, I said, Bata, Bata and I pointed and he looked down. *Oh, Ssues,* he said, his eyes shiny and black and wide opened like he just found out for the first time that he was wearing shoes. *Ssues...sssues...Saigon.* Yeah? I said, I guess I can't buy me some here in the good old U.S. of A then? Mine's Adidas. They're as old as Mrs. Hamilton, prehistoric if you ask me but they're still Adidas. A-di-das, go head, Kal, say it.

Adeedoos Sssues, Kal said, *Adeedoos.*

That's right, I said, very good, Kal. Adidas shoes. And yours, they're Bata shoes, and Kal said *theirs Bata sssues* and we both looked at each other and grinned like idiots and that's when Billy showed up. Why you want them gook shoes anyway, he said and cut in between us but nobody behind in line said noth-ing 'cause it's Billy. Why not, I said, trying to sound tough. Bata sounds kind of nice, Billy. They're from Saigon.

Bata sssues, the new kid said it again, trying to impress Billy.

But Billy wasn't impressed. My Daddy said them VCs don't wear shoes, he said. They wear sandals made from jeep tires and they live in fuck'n tunnels like moles and they eat bugs and snakes for lunch. Then afterwards they go up and take sniper shots at you with their AK-47s.

He don't look like he lived in no tunnel, I said.

Maybe not him, said Billy, but his Daddy I'm sure. Isn't that right, refugee boy? Your Daddy a VC? Your Daddy the one who gave my Daddy that goddamn scar?

The new kid didn't say nothing. You could tell he pretty much figured it out that Billy's an asshole 'cause you don't need no English for that. But all he could say was *no undohsten* and sssues *adeedoos* and those ain't no comeback lines and he knew it. So he just bit his lip and blushed and kept looking at me with them eyes.

So, I don't know why, maybe 'cause I didn't want him to know that I belonged to the c) category, or maybe 'cause he kept looking at me with those eyes, but I said leave him alone, Billy. I was kinda surprised that I said it. And Billy turned and looked at me like he was shocked too, like he just saw me for the first time or something. Then in this loud singsong voice, he said Bobby's protecting his new boyfriend. Everybody look, Bobby's got a boyfriend and he's gonna suck his VC's dick after lunch.

Everybody started to look.

The new kid kept looking at me like he was waiting to see what I was gonna do next. What I'd usually do next is shut my trap and pretend that I was invisible or try not to cry like last time when Billy got me in a headlock in the locker room and called me sissy over and over again 'cause I missed the softball in P.E. even when it was an easy catch. But not now. Now I couldn't pretend to be invisible 'cause too many people were looking. It was like I didn't have a choice. It was like now or never. So I said, you know what, Billy, don't mind if I do. I'm sure anything is bigger than yours and everybody in line said Ooohh.

Fuck you, you little faggot, Billy said.

No thanks, Billy, I said, I already got me a new boyfriend, remember?

Everybody said Ooohh again and Billy looked real mad. Then I got more scared than mad, my blood pumping. I thought oh my God, what have I done? I'm gonna get my lights punched out for sure. But then, God delivered stupid Becky. She suddenly stuck her beak in. And he's cute too she said, almost as cute as you, Bobby. A blond and a brunette. You two'll make a nice faggot couple, I'm sure. So like promise me you'll name your first born after me, OK?

So like I tore at her. That girl could never jump me, not in a zillion years. And I'm sure you're a slut, I said, I'm sure you'd couple with anything that moves. I'm sure there are litters of strayed mutts already named after you. You know, Bitch Becky One, Bitch Becky Two, and, let's not forget, Bow Wow Becky Junior and Becky called me asshole and looked away and everyone cracked up, even mean old Billy.

Man, he said, shaking his head, you got some mean mouth on you today. It was like suddenly I was too funny or famous for him to beat up. But after he bought his burger and chocolate milk, he said it real loud so everybody could hear, he said, I'll see you two bitches later. Outside.

Sure, Billy, I said and waved to him, see yah later, and then after we grabbed our lunch the new kid and me, we made a beeline for Mr. K.'s.

Boy, it was good to be in Mr. K.'s, I tell you. You don't have to watch over your shoulders every other second. You can play whatever game you want. Or you can read or just talk   So we ate and afterward I showed the new kid how to play speed. He was a quick learner too, if you asked me, but he lost pretty early on in the tournament. Then I lost too pretty damn quickly after him. So we sat around and I flipped through the X-Men comic book and tried to explain to the new kid why Wolverine is so cool 'cause he can heal himself with his mutant factor and he had claws that cut through metal, and Phoenix, she's my favorite, Phoenix's so very cool 'cause she can talk to you psychically and she knows how everybody feels without even having to ask them, and best of all, she can lift an eighteen-wheeler truck with her psycho-kinetic energy. That's way cool, don't you think, Kal. The new kid, he listened and nodded to everything I said like he understood. Anyway, after a while, there were more losers than winners and the losers surrounded us and interrogated the new kid like he was a POW or something.

You ever shoot anybody, Cao Long?

Did you see anybody get killed?

How *long* you been here Long? (Haha).

I hear they eat dogs over there, is that true? Have you ever eaten a dog?

Have you ever seen a helicopter blown up like in the movies?

No undohsten, the new kid answered to each question and smiled or shook his head or waved his hands like shooing flies but the loser flies wouldn't shoo. I mean where else could they go? Mr. K.'s was it. So the new kid looked at me again with them eyes and I said, OK, OK, Kal, I'll teach you something else. Why don't you say Hey, fuckheads, leave me alone! Go head, Kal, say it.

Hey-fuck-heads, I said, looking at him.

Hee, Foock headss, he said, looking at me.

Leave. Me. Alone! I said.

Leevenme olone! he said. Hee, *Foock headss. Leevenme olone!*

And everybody laughed. I guess that was the first time they got called fuckheads and actually felt good about it, but Mr. K. said Robert Quentin Mitchell, you watch your mouth or you'll never come in here again but you could tell he was trying not to laugh himself. So I said OK, Mr. K., but I leaned over and whispered *hey fuckheads, leave me alone* again in the new kid's ear so he'd remember and he looked at me like I'm the coolest guy in the world. Sthankew Rowbuurt, he said.

Then after school when I was waiting for my bus, the new kid found me. He gave me a folded piece of paper and before I could say anything he blushed and ran away. You'd never guess what it was. It was a drawing of me and it was really really good. I was smiling in it. I looked real happy and older, like a sophomore or something, not like in the 7th grade yearbook picture where I looked so goofy with my eyes closed and everything and I had to sign my name over it so people wouldn't look. When I got home I taped it on my family-tree chart and pinned the chart on my bedroom door and, I swear, the whole room had this vague eucalyptus smell.

Next day at Show and Tell Billy made the new kid cry. He went after Jimmy. Jimmy was this total nerd with thick glasses who told us how very challenging it was doing the New York Times crossword puzzles 'cause you got to know words like ubiquitous and undulate and capricious, totally lame and bogus stuff like that. When he took so long just to do five across and seven horizontal we shot spitballs at him and Mr. K. said stop that. But we got rid of that capricious undulating bozo ubiquitously fast and that was when Billy came up and made the new kid cry.

He brought in his Daddy's army uniform and a stack of old magazines. He unfolded the uniform with the name Baxter sewed under U.S. ARMY and put it on a chair. Then he opened one magazine and showed a picture of this naked and bleeding little girl running and crying on this road while these houses behind her were on fire. That's Napalm, he said, and it eats into your skin and burns for a long, long time. This girl, Billy said, she got burned real bad, see there, yeah. Then he showed another picture of this monk sitting cross-legged and he was on fire and everything and there were people standing behind him crying but nobody tried to put the poor man out. That's what you call self-immolation, Billy said. They do that all the time in 'Nam. This man, he poured gasoline on himself and lit a match 'cause he didn't like the government. Then Billy showed another picture of dead people in black pajamas along this road and he said these are VCs and my Daddy got at least a dozen of them before he was wounded himself. My Daddy told me if it weren't for them beatniks and hippies we could have won, Billy said, and that's when the new kid buried his face in his arms and cried and I could see his skinny shoulders go up and down like waves.

That's enough, Billy Baxter, Mr. K. said, you can sit down now, thank you.

Oh, man! Billy said, I didn't even get to the part about how my Daddy got his scar, that's the best part.

Never mind, Mr. K. said, sit down, please. I'm not sure whether you understood the assignment but you were supposed to do an oral presentation on what you've done or something that has to do with you, a hobby or a personal project, not the atrocities your father committed in Indochina. Save those stories for when you cruise the bars when you're old enough.

Then Mr. K. looked at the new kid like he didn't know what to do next. That war, he said, I swear. After that it got real quiet in the room and all you could hear was the new kid sobbing. Cao, Mr. K. said finally, real quiet like, like he didn't really want to bother him. Cao, are you all right? Cao Long Nguyen?

The new kid didn't answer Mr. K. so I put my hand on his shoulder and shook it a little. Hey, Kal, I said, you OK?

Then it was like I pressed an ON button or something, 'cause all of a sudden Kal raised his head and stood up. He looked at me and then he looked at the blackboard. He looked at me again, then the blackboard. Then he marched right up there even though it was Roger's turn next and Roger, he already brought his two pet snakes and everything. But Kal didn't care. Maybe he thought it was his turn 'cause Mr. K. called his name and so he just grabbed a bunch of colored chalk from Mr. K.'s desk and started to draw like a wild man and Mr. K. he let him.

We all stared.

He was really really good but I guess I already knew that.

First he drew a picture of a boy sitting on this water buffalo and then he drew this rice field in green. Then he drew another boy on another water buffalo and they seemed to be racing. He drew other kids running along the bank with their kites in the sky and you could tell they were laughing and yelling, having a good time. Then he started to draw little houses on both sides of this river and the river ran toward the ocean and the ocean had big old waves. Kal drew a couple standing outside this very nice house holding hands and underneath them Kal wrote *Ba* and *Ma*. Then he turned and looked straight at me, his eyes still wet with tears. *Rowbuurt*, he said, tapping the pictures with his chalk, his voice sad but expecting, *Rowbuurt*.

Me? I said. I felt kinda dizzy. Everybody was looking back and forth between him and me now like we were tossing a softball between us or something.

Rowbuurt. Kal said my name again and kept looking at me until I said what, what'd you want, Kal?

Kal tapped the blackboard with his chalk again and I saw in my head the picture of myself taped on my family-tree and then I don't know how but I just kinda knew. So I just took a deep breath and then I said, OK, OK, Kal, uhmm, said he used to live in this village with his Mama and Papa near where the river runs into the sea, and Kal nodded and smiled and waved his chalk in a circle like he was saying *Go on, Robert Quentin Mitchell, you're doing fine, go on.*

So I went on.

And he went on.

I talked. He drew.

We fell into a rhythm.

He had a good time racing them water buffaloes with his friends and flying kites, I said. His village is, hmm, very nice, and...and...and...at night he goes to sleep swinging on this hammock and hearing the sound of the ocean behind the dunes and everything.

Then one day, I said, the soldiers named VCs came with guns and they took his Daddy away. They put him behind barbed wire with other men, all very skinny, skinny and hungry and they got chains on their ankles and they looked really, really sad. Kal and his mother went to visit his Daddy and they stood on the other side of the fence and cried a lot. Yes, it was very, very sad. Then, hmm, one day his Daddy disappeared. No, he didn't disappear, he died, he died.

And Kal and his mother buried him in this cemetery with lots of graves and they lit candles and cried and cried. After that, there was this boat, this really crowded boat, I guess, and Kal and his Mama climbed on it and they went down the river out to sea. Then they got on this island and then they got on an airplane after that and they came here to live in America.

Kal was running out of space. He drew the map of America way too big but he didn't want to erase it. So he climbed on a chair and drew these high-rises right above the rice fields and I recognized the Trans-American building right away, a skinny pyramid underneath a rising moon. Then he drew a big old heart around it. Then he went back to the scene where the man named Ba who stood in the doorway with his wife and he drew a heart around him. Then he went back to the first scene of the two boys racing on the water buffaloes in the rice field and paused a little before he drew tiny tennis shoes on the boys' feet and I heard Billy say that's Bobby and his refugee boyfriend but I ignored him.

Kal loves America very much, especially San Francisco, I said, he'd never seen so many tall buildings before in his whole life and they're so pretty. Maybe he'll live with his mother someday up in the penthouse when they have lots of money. But he misses home too and he misses his friends and he especially misses his Daddy who died. A lot. And that's all, I said. I think he's done, thank you.

And he was done. Kal turned around and climbed down from the chair. Then he looked at everybody and checked out their faces to see if they understood. Then in this real loud voice he said, *Hee, Foock headss, leevenme olone!* and bowed to them and everybody cracked up and applauded.

Kal started walking back. He was smiling and looking straight at me with his teary eyes like he was saying *Robert Quentin Mitchell, ain't we a team or what?* and I wanted to say yes, yes, Kal Long Nguyen—Refugee, yes we are but I just didn't say anything.

The Dead

Linh Dinh

The nine-year-old hockey puck
Bounced from the fender of an olive truck
Now bounces a leather ball on his forehead.
The old lady who scrounged potted meat
From foreign men lying in a mortar pit
Now sells gold jewelry in Santa Barbara.
The dead are not dead but wave at pretty strangers
From their pick-up trucks on Bolsa Avenue.
They sit at Formica tables smoking discount cigarettes.
Some have dyed their hair, changed their name to Bill.
But the living, some of them, like to dig up the dead,
Dress them in native costumes, shoot them again,
Watch their bodies rise in slow motion.

Know by Heart

Trinh T. Minh-ha

Know by Heart

the worst thing
I'll have to recite this
twice a day
the worst thing
is to give
meaning to
something that
hasn't got
any

Ecstasied

touching
living
the ecstasy
of an in-
finite moment
when riveted
lost bemused
in-timately
looking at
listening to
radiates
like a sweet madness

Drunk in the motions of the look
while the world tiptoes nearby

Looking at the Dream Screen

savoring
inhaling your presence purblind
enraptured by the closeness
our bodies hardly body
unable to hear taste see
while other lives unfold on the screen
a dream within dream after dream
that suspends bends
every minute spent side by side
mesmerized as if by the same
images

sapid
sa-a-ppy
sit and see
but save the tongue
afterall
can I how can I reach out
with words
when touching I can't never
can feel all
I ever feel is the dumb
sleeve of your shirt

violent forceful obstinate
so it seems with desire
whose power and excess
never fail thoughtless
to mistake wander for wonder
so when a dream in the dark
awakens our moonless bodies
life makes its demands
hitting where it hurts
engulfing all emotions
pretending it knows
how love through bondage
can be lodged in language

The Frame

fragile
the grace of a frame
becoming distinct to the touch
vulner ability is
a caress

The Flare

a pain so intense

curl
sucked up
by a void
consumed
by anger
coil

a spell so intense

cut cursed
a visceral need
to fight
however felt

The Cry

no
not a single day
passes by
without this strange cry

is that it?

First Night

first night at your place
even thick walls have your eyes
even alone I feel shy

first night in your space
doors closed rooms apart
ten walls no wall between us

Wordwarring

wordcaresses
you always point with
your eyes
wordarrows
you react with
markers mines missiles
while laughing
in spite of myself
I take them in
stinging
burning
bleeding
at a loss

That voice

subject to vertigo
hit and sick at heart
I went on speaking
as if
untouched
nothing had happened
there
unmoved
stones
stoned in my throat
even I
couldn't recognize
that coarsened voice
wounded love had found

Scent of Musk

with time
I often wonder
how she fares

today
every nuance
in That voice
crazes her
like the unbearable
(impossible to love)
lustily persistent
(impossible to forget)
scent of musk
every time I hear it
I want to hit that door open
cross that senseless wall
with the savage passion of...

a wounded animal
knowing only
how to fling itself
straight at the man
who gives it pain

today
That absence
sets the landscape
afire
with melancholia
and her insides
burn down to ashes
then
sometimes I stop
breathing
as I walk down a street
feeling the sun
flowering on my face
so fiery hot
so blinding clear
it hurts

the short stay left its mark
as I now stare out
so strangely
at the familiar horizon
the sea down the hill
framing neatly
the distant cityscape

Casual Letter

Sometimes I'd rather see your look than your eyes. If I were to tell the story I would remember only this. In the aftermath of the collision they were, for a second, wordlessly exchanging looks. Caressing...no, fleetingly making love with their...eyes. There the story would stop. The rest becomes so blurred in my mind that if I continue I will have to divagate again into the open field of the mind's eye. The incident was unreal. I was unreal, light. Trying to prevent both confusion and lucidity to kill desire. Responses in words wavered pathetically between saying too much and saying nothing. In its demands for sensual attentiveness passion turns words into toads, making it impossible to venture into speaking without withdrawing speech. The splinters of a casual accident shattered the play of our dreaming bodies, leading me back to the open field of the mind's eye.... It may not be deliberate but it often turned out to be sillily effective. The way you sometimes smashed the intense feeling of quiet festivity raised by your...patiently giving taking presence. Even in the very tenuous contact of the voice. Or in the interstices of it, where I caught in between two sentences a glimpse of a body accessed down to its guts. A sigh, a wordless exclamation, a sound comma, an onomatopoeia of the heart.... The way you hardly reciprocate with the same, sorry, sickness. The lonely experience of disappointment and senseless anguish you succeed in generating always without your knowing it. Your casualness and apparent disengagement from all obsessive, excessive feelings. "Suffering a bit," as you would say, as I am to remain at once monstrous in my demands and defenseless to the slightest injuries. A strange kind of suffering when no one is physically hurt. Constantly led to question the way I am, and I can't bear what I am in this twilight zone of reflection and emotion, I find myself measuring every giving gesture. Mine. Stop reacting with the skin. Mine. In my faulty moves I can blame only myself. Me. Imagination is held captive and ordered to come to an abrupt stop in its wild activities. Now when you affirm, I remain silent. Falling twice over, foolishly. For how could I fix my eyes on yours while searching for their look? Today I find myself puzzling instead, over the degree of their...intensity. How true? How far? What's in? You'll never give up yourself entirely, so you casually said. How true. The story goes that a beggar man thus spoke to a beggar woman: why do you ask for so much? To which the woman answered, why not, why not ask for more? I thought I'd never known her before, but here I am loving her who can, even when she can no longer

It Went By Me

something very beautiful
just went by me
something not to tell
in words in feelings
so fragile so wild
something yet to tell
is no longer
why and when it left
i can't tell

from **Monkey Bridge**
Lan Cao

Bedrooms are dangerous places. Insomniacs cultivate their clandestine selves there; mothers unload their burdens and hoard intricate sheddings; and interlopers like me go to unearth other people's secrets. My mother's bedroom was dark, emptied of her. A goosenecked lamp scowled from the corner, leaking a meek twenty watts' worth of light into the room. My mother found the dark reassuring. She enjoyed this, the sunset, the vacant streets, dusk seeping through the blinds, bleeding long narrow sheets of gray against the pock-marked floors. I threw myself on her bed and felt the seemingly infinite silence, the expanse of sadness that was peculiarly hers, dissolve inside my body. I had gone into her bedroom with the best of intentions, looking for two new sets of clothes to take to the hospital. "The red and pink pajamas at the bottom of the third drawer of my bedroom chest, counting from the bottom up," she had instructed.

My mother had a routine, a special brand of night language I had learned to expect. In my bedroom, huddled next to hers, I waited as she made her way across the creaky floors into the unlit bathroom. The sound of water flowing through the pipes settled like a hazy film over the stillness of five minutes past midnight. A few minutes passed, and she retraced her steps toward the door, sidled softly onto the bed, and—click—turned on the bedside lamp.

Once or twice, when I happened upon her in the middle of the night, I'd caught her off guard, half asleep, with her papers spilling from her arms. My mother could be a fugitive even in her own home. She had an instinctive distrust for everyone, which was why I assumed she always went down the stairway and through the cement corridor to throw her papers into the trash compactor in the early morning, before the trash men came.

It wasn't her fault that she'd forgotten her bedroom was a catacomb of recesses in which secrets could be hidden and later found. Here I was, among stray objects she called hers—an old swivel-neck fan, a threadbare towel, a pair of brown slippers. If I were the kind of person who believed in the spirit world, I would describe the feeling as that of someone who had come upon the presence of an enormous ghost, a strange lingering presence that induced a quickening of the pulse. I ran my fingers across the pages, common notepad paper from the local dime store, crowded with columns of black ink. There was my mother's handwriting. I could trace its movements, the deep strokes, the fine, deft lines. Its muscular letters, erect and vertical, marched across the creased pages in a formal, authoritative Vietnamese I could still read and understand but could not, at this point, write myself. I took a deep gulp of air and watched myself contemplate the possibility of touching, actually touching, this untouchable part of my mother's nighttime life.

Mai doesn't believe in the magic that's locked in my ears. She doesn't know that the story of my ears is the same as the story of my mother's life in the rice-growing province of Ba Xuyen. Of course I wasn't born yet, because the story of my ears begins on my mother's wedding day, the day her parents married her to Baba Quan.

In the splashy, sunny morning after the monsoon season, in the province of Ba Xuyen in the Mekong Delta, my mother, Tuyet, fourteen years old at the time, filled two big buckets of water from the river and hitched them onto two ends of a pole, hauled the pole onto her right shoulder, and began the long trek back to the house, ready for the bustling activities of that day.

It was the morning of her wedding day. In the span of one hour my mother had to do her chores, she had to have been as limber as a carp to move swiftly across the fields without spilling a drop of water. She hurried home and scrubbed the front steps to the little house. This was the spot where she and her parents would stand to greet the groom later that day.

Bright wedding-red flowers in full bloom stood cloistered on the steps. It was the beginning of a new day, and there were great hopes for my mother's new life. Nearby, water buffaloes in the field wallowed in muddy ditches flooded by fresh rainwater, tadpoles in the lotus pond in the back learned how to croak, banana trees pummeled into hunchbacks by the torrential rain gingerly straightened their spines, and bougainvilleas budding purple and blinding pink began wiggling their way back up the walls.

Never had it been cold enough in Ba Xuyen for my mother to see snow—flowers from a white heaven, as the villagers called it—for which she was named. Other girls in her village were named after indigenous flowers or called simply by the order of their birth, but her father thought she was rare and special and would do unexpected things, so he named her after snow, "Tuyet." Her name had been inspired by a winter picture of a bucolic French country scene. It wasn't a name any French aristocrat would name his daughter, nor was it a beautiful name for an Annamite peasant girl. But my grandfather doted on her, gave her a distinctive name, and threw a big traditional one-month anniversary celebration in her honor. Well-wishers from the village came in crowds. Her mother displayed her proudly in a small cradle for everyone to see, her reddish and wrinkled face painted with circles of cinnabar, a magic drug to deter evil spirits from jealousy. Perhaps because of her unusual name, my mother was different even at that age, more active, more fierce, the villagers said, even than most baby boys. A fighting fish, they used to call her.

"It can get so cold that their breath does acrobatics in the air just to keep warm. It can get so cold that dragons have to blow fire into the sun so hard their scales drop off. It can get so cold that their monsoon dares not appear, and my Tuyet would have to be dispatched in its stead," my grandfather would boast about his daughter's name.

She was his precious little girl, but even precious little girls had to be married off. And so my mother's wedding day had been more or less predetermined, probably on the very day she was born. The morning of her wedding began uneventfully. Her parents had arranged the family altar hours before. The three incense sticks stuck in a bowl of rice were burning steadily to their bones. The porcelain cups of chrysanthemum tea rested solemnly on the silk brocade. And sweets prepared weeks in advance—candied coconuts sliced into paper-thin strips, ginger diced into thick cubes and coated with rock sugar, tamarinds dipped in syrup to give them a succulent sour taste that tickled the tongue—were proudly displayed on the bamboo table. My mother gave the dirt path a last-minute sweep. Their chickens and ducks and pigs had been herded without protest into the wire pens. The groom's dowry, two soaped-down pink pigs, hunched together in a corner while the family's pigs stared territorial warnings at them.

At noon, when the sun was big and round and directly overhead, my mother watched the procession toward her house of men with trays draped in red cloth and gold tassels. The groom, Baba Quan, held in his hands a platter of betel nut and betel leaves and lime paste—traditional wedding arrangement that signified everlasting fidelity and love. Along the wedding route, girls with their baby brothers and sisters straddled against their hips watched the ritual from their front steps. Even the earth, replenished by months of monsoon water, rumbled festively under the renewed activities of tadpoles and bougainvilleas. And so the wedding ceremony began and ended with my mother and father performing the requisite three bows before the altar.

That night, in the black stupor of her husband's house, in a village three full days and nights away by horse-drawn carriage, my mother lay lifeless and rigid, against a bed of bleached white cotton, whiter and purer than tuyet—snow— itself. The following morning, fresh blood, three drops, and redder than the red mixture released from a betel-nut roll, dotted the pristine landscape of white. The morning after that, in full fanfare, to my mother's astonishment and fear, she found herself seated in a freshly painted carriage being driven along the winding dirt path back to her family house.

Although she didn't know it then, red had become a life fluid for my mother and her family. My mother was returning to her village, fortunately, as an accidental victor in a very old war. Old men and women lined the dirt street and cheered as her wagon passed by. In their hands, strips of white cloth large as bedsheets waved like miniature flags hoisted by a conquered land. An open cart with a red roasted pig led the way, its two plump ears proudly intact, triangular and solid like pyramids pointing at the sky—thanks to the red virginal blood of the wedding night. Along the route, people cried "Tuyet is home," "Tuyet is home," and "The pig has two ears," "The pig has two ears." The moment my grandparents saw the pig's uncut ears, they quickly dropped to their knees and knelt gratefully before the family altar.

They had not warned my mother beforehand of the possible doom that might befall the family had she not been able to produce the three drops of blood on her wedding night. Fear and anxiety, they had heard, may cause all the blood, even in a virginal body, to gather in the brain, in which case there might not be any left for the wedding night.

They remembered only too well what had happened many years ago to another village girl. She was "all white and no red," as people said, like a rotten egg with too much white and not enough yolk. Her husband's family had thrown her on an old wagon, the kind used to cart animals and dead wood. Next to her, hanging from a pole pierced through its body, was a giant roasted pig, both its ears shamefully shorn into two little stumps.

When the wagon passed their house, the villagers had thrown rocks at the wagon and spat in the girl's direction. Several village elders chased after the cart and cursed her karma with hexes they claimed would last generation after generation.

That night, villagers torched the family's barn and drove all their farm animals and livestock into the fields. Flames leapt into the air, lapping up everything with their fiery tongues. With sledgehammers and scythes, the villagers slashed every animal in sight, and the flesh that hung from the carcasses bled pools of red into the soil. The next morning, the body of the bride was found by an old stream, her blood turning the water the bright color of her wedding-red dress. Even the village notables, the keepers of village order and morality, had had to denounce the incident as lawless and excessive.

All the animals were killed, except the pigs. The pigs were spared, so that their ears could be slashed as a warning to bad daughters who ventured beyond the traditional circle of virtue. The next day, a band of pigs without ears could be seen running like lost souls wailing mournful wails that could be heard several villages away.

For reparation, the groom's family naturally got back everything—every box of tea, every roll of fabric, every mother-of-pearl pin—they had previously presented as dowry.

My mother did not know any of this that day when she left the village with her new husband. She only knew, upon her return, when my grandmother told her, that she had escaped a disaster greater than the fiercest of monsoons—the red wedding-night stains had declared triumphantly the modest fact of her purity. There were many shades of red, my mother was told, the angry red of bursting vessels, the blushing red of a modest young girl, the prosperous red of lucky paper, the wedding red of a traditional wedding dress, the bloody explosive red of war, *and of course the proud red of virginal blood. My mother, her mother whispered, had avoided acquaintance with the deathly versions.*

What did my mother's wedding day have to do with my ear? One year after the triumphant celebration held in my mother's honor, she gave birth to a baby girl, me. My mother was not like other girls in Ba Xuyen. Born in the scalding heat of the equator, she had, after all, been named after snow. And so she was by nature rebellious. And I became the perfect expression of her rebellion.

The moment I was born, I was already blessed with long, Buddha-shaped ears, so long that the rest of my face had to grow into them. "Push, push," my mother's midwife had yelled, her hands reaching inside to pull, pull, pull me by the head into the world. But as the midwife later told me, it was my ears, my long, long ears that the midwife had touched, and it was by the ears that I was first tugged from my mother's womb. It was also with my magical ears that I could immediately hear gasps and sighs of the startled neighbors who had gathered to watch the event of my birth. My ears, everyone must have noticed, were almost two times as big as my little newborn face. How many other people in this world can remember the sounds of their birth?

My ears, according to my mother, were ears reborn and made permanently whole to compensate for the stumps of pig ears that had been inflicted genera-tionally on the girls of our village. Inside my ears were the rage and revenge of every girl from every generation before whose return with a shameful and earless pig had destroyed her family's lives—lives my mother had now gloriously resur-rected. For every custom the village notables considered harmless and natural under the name of tradition, a pair of supernatural ears would be born to coun-teract such a belief, my mother whispered. Through my ears, my mother pro-claimed, I would have the power not only to heal my mother's fear but also to repair generation after generation of past wrongs by healing the faces of karma itself.

My ears, in fact, were an event so rare, so momentous, that the villagers, some holding strings of beads, others banging on drums, immediately hired for-tune-tellers and astrologers, who reached deep into their starry vault to chart my life. That was why I was named Thanh, for the clarity and brilliance that my ears would bring to the family—and, as the villagers hastily added, to the entire vil-lage as well.

My ears continued to grow longer and longer every day, until one day they looked like Siddhartha Gautama's ears on the day he attained enlightenment. The villagers called them heavenly ears. Notables came by to show my mother pictures of the Buddha. They compared my ears to his, long and slender and spanning from temples to chin. Acupuncturists told my mother about passages in ancient Chinese textbooks that described the ear as a miracle organ, a curled-up fetus that contained every anatomical point in its membranes. In the ear, they said, lay all the healing powers of the world. A needle inserted in a specific point on the fetal-shaped ear would invoke energy flows in a corresponding point located in another part of the human body, bringing back to balance the visceral organs causing the physical disorder in the first place.

There is power in these ears, the power to redeem and the power to avenge. And so my mother believed. I trust whatever I pick up with my ears. They have become my very own radar. With them, I can prevent bloodshed and protect our family's honor. Through my ears, my mother was able to reclaim the consummation ceremony as her own, to ensure that her fate would never be determined by the length of something as humiliating as a pig's ears ever again.

Mai would not believe the story about my ears even if I were to tell her directly. She still talks to me as if I make no sense. Not so loud, Mom, she whispers. Everything that smells of life before, my daughter thinks she can scour clean. She has disengaged and unremembered so swiftly something as big as a life, disassembling it from her mind as if it had never been.

She believes she has to go away to learn. She tells me that it's the American way. College is the American equivalent of the Shaolin Temple and the bo tree and the emperor's court and other, similar nonsense. But really it's the Vietnamese way, my Vietnamese way, that's made me go along with her story, that's made me feel sorry for this child of mine, so lost between two worlds that she can't find her way back onto the veins and the arteries of her mother's love. We come from a culture of subtlety. She wants me to let her walk blamelessly out of one life and into another. And that was my gift to her, to allow her the satisfaction of thinking I'm unaware. Because I know the real reason she wants to leave. It's my face, the face of her mother, her very own face, from which she wants to flee.

How can I teach her that the worthwhile enterprise is the enterprise of learn-

ing to live with our scars? She hates imperfection, she doesn't like to look at anything blemished. She looks at her mother's black tropical cottons and sees Vietcong pajamas. She looks at her mother's face and sees scars, takes it for a sign of damage, not a badge of survival. Tender flesh the color of pearls makes her cringe.

Her own mother, the one she sees as obsolete and defective, is a woman who's gone through more wars that she'll ever know, who's maneuvered through more cultures than I hope she'll ever have to negotiate, who's memorized book after book of Baudelaire and Moliere and Verlaine. This woman is a woman she views with suspicion, and for what reason? Because her mother, who has had to learn Chinese and French, and master them better than a Pekingese and a Parisian, speaks English with an accent? Because her mother has a face that's been sawed and planed and chiseled and varnished under layers of finish that's not finished enough for her?

Only from her American teachers can she acquire knowledge, she believes, only from their fountain can she drink the holy water. Not from her mother, who has been an exile many times over, starting with the day I was plucked from the nuns of the Providence School at fifteen to immigrate to her father's house in a village one hundred kilometers away, a house full of strangers and strange rules I had to learn in order to be the best daughter-in-law her grandmother had ever seen.

Who better to teach her to listen for things that have yet to occur than her own mother, who predicted before any political pundit the demise of the French colonial empire in Indochina, at a then little-known place called Dien Bien Phu? I know an omen when I see one, and when the French yelled "Dien Bien Phu, Dien Bien Phu," as if they were yelling "Tiennent Bien Fous, tiennent bien fous"—Hang on, you dopes, hang on, you dopes—I knew it was a subconscious realization that the ineluctable end for them was soon to come.

I remember the way things were between us. How she used to listen, those nights when her father had gone off to make a name for himself as the intellectual whose radical ideas would lead Vietnam into the modern age. We would sit alone on the bench overlooking a mango grove. Her cheeks were soft and tender like ripe coconut flesh pressed against my breasts. Her eyes wide and solicitous and framed by jet-black lashes I made thick and long by trimming the ends every few months. With her arms looped around my neck, she felt so fragile and small. I wanted to shield her from evil and provide for her every need. I was a mother in love with my child, and the urge to hang on to her forever was a hunger no one but a mother could understand.

She loved my stories then. The story of the kingdom of Champa, the story of an entire country's karma.

No one can escape the laws of karma. Nor can a country divest itself of the karmic consequences of its own actions. That's why I wasn't totally surprised by what's happened to us as a country. For every action there is a reaction, for every deed of destruction there is a consequence. It's something as exact and implacable as the laws of physics. No Vietnamese has dared forget the destruction of Champa. None of us can ignore the total demolition of Indrapura and the thousands and thousands of Chams by our ancestors when we expanded southward. My mother, may she rest in peace, once took me to the beautiful ruins the Chams had built in their glory days. She did it not to scare me, but to teach me the facts of life. And as I sit here in the middle of the night and look at us now, a people and a country utterly abandoned, utterly destroyed, it is not bewildered tears I weep, not at all. We all knew what we did to the Chams was an omen of things to come, of karma wrought and karma returned.

Karma is the antithesis of the Manifest Destiny, the kind of Manifest Destiny they teach my daughter in her history book about the great American West. Ours is not a nation of pioneers. I truly don't understand the American preoccupation with cowboys who win and Indians who lost. It must be the American sense of invincibility, like a child's sense that nothing she does can possibly have real consequences. Our southward expansion we study with sorrow and shame, not with a sense of conquest and pride. Karma is based less on rights and entitlements than on moral duty and obligation, less on celebration of victories than on repentance and atonement.

But my Vietnamese-born daughter would never accept this way of thinking. The world to her is a new frontier, clean, pristine, ready to be molded and shaped by any pair of skillful and pioneering hands. "You are what your parents say you are. You are what your ancestors were a hundred years ago." These are things she rebels against. She wrinkles up her nose and makes a face when I try to give her the real gems of life. She thinks I am a mystifier out to confuse her world, to make her see double where there are only simple mathematical answers. But to release her into a world whose secret workings she refuses to recognize is something a mother can never do. Because what danger is more dangerous than danger unacknowledged—and in my daughter's case danger scornfully considered, danger taunted, then dismissed?

When Mai was seven years old, on the anniversary of a Vietnamese victory against yet another Chinese invasion, I showed her a picture of the majestic river where our forces defeated the enemy and turned their warships belly-up like panic-stricken turtles trapped in the sand.

"The Chinese once deployed a giant fleet of armored junks on this river," I said. "Our people drove iron-tipped spikes into the riverbed and lured the enemy convoy up the river at high tide, when the stakes were invisible. When the Chinese vessels, big and heavy like overbloated whales, were all upstream, we waited until the tide ebbed before we retreated. Our boats were small and nimble, and we moved easily through the water. The more we retreated, the more they pursued, the more entrapped they became, impaled and immobilized, a perfect target for our troops."

This was a lesson on what not to do. Watch out for iron stakes beneath a beautiful, calm surface, I explained. She laughed and clapped, delighted that her mother was giving her one more jewel to hold and rub in her palm. And I of course held her in my arms like a craftswoman awed by the beauty and intricacy of an object she had somehow herself created.

The same advice my daughter now rejects as bad fortune-cookie advice. She stares, her head tilted, her eyes narrowed, pretending to decipher the hidden wisdom that her eyes tell me she doesn't believe. How has it come to this? How have I failed to retrieve my own daughter from the stranger she has become?

During our old, haunted nights by the mango grove, we had our routines, games of emperor and peasant I hoped my daughter would learn to appreciate and play.

"Once upon a time," I would begin, "when the Chinese governor, a chess champion, proposed a chess match between himself and our emperor to test our *national learning, the emperor, who was not a chess player, knew he had to come up with a plan to save face, his and the nation's. After an exhaustive search through every hamlet and village, the emperor's soldiers discovered a peasant who was a brilliant player. The peasant told the emperor to agree to the match, on the condition that it begin at noon. The peasant then donned military uniform and became one of the emperor's guards, standing behind him with a giant parasol to protect from the dead-noon heat, which could be as fierce, as sharp as a column of red ants on bare skin. This parasol had been pierced beforehand with a giant hole through which only one minuscule ray of sunlight could pass. By tilting the parasol and moving it in such a way as to illuminate the precise piece the emperor should move, the peasant was able to shepherd the emperor's play and guide him toward victory, saving the country from yet another Chinese invasion."*

All my daughter's life, I have played the part of this peasant, pointing my magic finger so my daughter will know which route to follow, shining my light on her bishops, her knights, her pawns, preempting attacks from the other side's invisible soldiers, teaching her how to protect her king and queen. But my daughter no longer watches or listens to me because I am no longer the guide she looks to for her voyage across the chess board, I must teach her everything she needs to know to make that trip someday on her own.

And most of all, I must give her the ears with which I was born, a set of ears so miraculous that they contain all the other senses combined. Ears that can not only hear inaudible sound waves, but see, like a falcon, the most minute flea from far above, that can feel even the smallest change in atmospheric equilibrium, that can unmask the rhythmless rhythm of danger and betrayal and strip open the stenchless guiles of a two-faced face, ears so keen they can sense through the thickest fogs, smell the faintest scent; taste the flavor of poison on another's breath; distinguish the pungent zest of a grain of salt from the honey-sweetness of a grain of sugar without either grain's touching the tongue. Those are precisely the kinds of ears my mother gave me.

My awesome ears, that's what I want to pass down to my daughter.

M.I.A.

Bao-Long Chu

When you come back,
don't bother to

go to Cho Lon.
I am not there
among mangoes

I once peddled.
I am here now:

America.
Yes, I wait still.
Still, as Buddha.

I wake early
daily to make

you lotus soup
you love, thinking
you will today

break down this house
when you come back

and find me, love
breaking, broken
into ashes.

The green seas stretch
but they're not end-

less. If you are
lost, please follow
my skin, my faith.

I burn nightly.

Grandma's Tales

Andrew Lam

The day after Mama and Papa took off to Las Vegas, Grandma died. Nancy and I, we didn't know what to do. Vietnamese traditional funerals with incense sticks and chanting Buddhist monks not being our thing. We have a big freezer, Nancy said. Why don't we freeze her. Really. Why bother Mama and Papa—what's another day or two for Grandma now anyway?

Nancy's older than me, and since I didn't have any better idea, we iced her.

Grandma was ninety-four years, eight months, and six days old when she died. She lived through three wars, two famines, and a full hard life. America, besides, was not all that good for her. She had been confined to the second floor of our big Victorian home, as her health was failing, and she did not speak English, only a little French, like *Oui Monsieur, c'est évidemment un petit monstre,* and *Non, Madame, vous n'êtes pas du tout enceinte, je vous assure.* She was a head nurse in the maternity ward of the Hanoi hospital during the French colonial time. I used to love her stories about delivering all these strange two-headed babies and Siamese triplets connected at the hip whom she named Happy, Liberation, and Day.

Grandma's death came when she was eating spring rolls with me and Nancy. Nancy was wearing a nice black miniskirt and her lips were painted red, and Grandma said you look like a high-class whore. Nancy made a face and said she was preparing to go to one of her famous San Francisco artsy cocktail parties where waiters were better dressed than most upper-class Vietnamese men back home, and there were silver trays of duck pâté and salmon mousse, and ice sculptures with wings and live musicians playing Vivaldi. So get off my case, Grandma, and I'm no whore.

It was a compliment, Grandma said, winking at me, but I guess it's wasted on you, Child. Then, as Nancy prepared to leave, Grandma laughed and said, Child, do the cha-cha-cha for me. I didn't get to do it when I was young, with my clubbed foot and the wars and everything else.

Sure, Grandma, Nancy said, and rolled her pretty eyes.

That was when Grandma dropped her chopsticks on the hardwood floor—clack, clack, clatter, clack clack—closed her eyes, and stopped breathing. Just like that.

So we iced her. She was small enough that she fit right above the TV dinner trays and the frozen yogurt bars we were going to have for dessert. We wrapped all of grandma's five-foot-three, ninety-eight pound, lithe body in Saran Wrap and hoped Mama and Papa would get the Mama-Papa-come-home-quick-Grandma's-dead letter that we sent to Circus-Circus, where they were staying.

Meanwhile Nancy had a party to go to, and I had to meet Eric.

Eric's so cool. Eric has eyes so blue you can swim in them. Eric has this laugh that makes you warm all over. And Eric is really beautiful and a year older than me, a senior. And he liked Grandma a lot. Neither one knew the other's language, but there was this thing between them, mutual respect, like one cool old chic to a cool young dude. (Sometimes I would translate but not always 'cause my English is not all that good and my Vietnamese sucks.) What was so cool about Grandma was that she was the only one who knew I'm bisexual. Even though she was Confucian bound and trained and a Buddhist and all, she was really cool about it.

One night, we were sitting together in the living room watching a John Wayne movie called *The Green Berets*. And Eric was there with me and Grandma. (Mama and Papa had just gone to bed and Nancy was at some weird black and white ball or something like that.) And Eric leaned over and kissed me on the lips and Grandma said, that's real nice, and I translated and we all laughed and John Wayne shot dead five guys. Just like that. But Grandma didn't mind, really. She's seen Americans like John Wayne shooting her people in the movies before. She always thought of him as a bad guy, uglier than the water buffalo's ass. And she'd seen us more passionate than a kiss on the lips and didn't mind though she used to tell us to be careful and not make any babies—obviously a joke—'cause she's done delivering them. So you see, we liked Grandma a lot.

Anyway, we made out on the couch for a while then I said: Eric, I have to tell you something. Grandma's dead. You're kidding me, he said and smiled his beautiful smile like he didn't believe me. I kid you not, I said. She's dead, and Nancy and me, we iced her. Shit! Eric said, why? 'Cause if we didn't pack her in -12 Fahrenheit she would start to smell, duh, and we have to wait for my parents to perform a traditional Vietnamese funeral and everything.

Shit, Eric said again and then we both fell silent. After a while Eric said, can I take a peek at Grandma?

Sure, I said, sure you can, she was as much yours as she was mine, and we went to the freezer and looked in.

The weird thing was the freezer was on defrost and Grandma was nowhere in sight. But there was a trail of water and Saran Wrap leading from the freezer to her bedroom. So we held on to each other and followed it. On the bed, all wet and everything, sat Grandma, counting her Buddhist rosary and chanting her diamond sutra. What's weirder is that she looked real young. I mean around fifty-four now, not ninety-four, the high cheeks, the rosy lips. She smiled when she saw us and the she said: "What do you say we all go to one of those famous cocktail parties that Nancy's gone to, the three of us?" Now, I wasn't scared, she being my Grandma and all, but what really got me feeling all these goose bumps on my neck and arms was that she said it in English, I mean accentless, California English. I mean the way Mrs. Collier, our neighbor, the English teacher speaks English. Me, I have a slight accent still but Grandma's was really fine.

Wow, Grandma, said Eric, your English is excellent and you look like a babe.

I know, Grandma said, winking at him, that's just the side benefit of being reborn. But enough with the compliments, Son, we got to party.

Cool, said Eric.

Cool, I said, though I was a bit jealous 'cause I had to go through junior high and high school and take all those damn ESL classes and everything to learn the same language and Grandma just got it down cold—no pun intended. Grandma went to her closet and picked out a nice brocade red blouse and a pair of black silk pants and a pair of sequined velvet shoes then she fixed her hair real nice, and then we drove off downtown.

Boy, you should've seen Nancy's face when we came in. I mean she nearly tripped over herself and had to put her face on the wing of this ice sculpture that looked like a big melting duck to calm herself. Then she walked straight up to us, all haughty like and said, It's invitation only, how'd y'all get in?

Calm yourself, Child, said Grandma. I told them that I was a board member of the Cancer Society and flashed my jade bracelet here and diamond ring and gave the man a forty-dollar tip. And Nancy had the same reaction Eric and I had: Grandma, your English, it's flawless!

But Grandma was oblivious to compliments. She went straight to the punch bowl to scoop up some spirits. That's when I noticed that her clubbed foot was cured, and she had this new elegant grace about her. She drifted, you might say, across the room, her hair floating like gray-black clouds behind her, and everyone stared, mesmerized.

Needless to say Grandma was the big hit of the artsy-fartsy party. She had so many interesting stories to tell. The feminists, it seemed, loved her the most. They crowded around her like hens around a barnyard rooster and made it hard for the rest of us to hear her. But Grandma told her stories all right. She told them how she'd been married early and had eight children while being the patriarch of the middle-class family during the Viet Minh uprising. She told them about my grandfather, a brilliant man who was well versed in Molière and Shakespeare and who was an accomplished violinist but who drank himself to death 'cause he felt helpless against the colonial powers of the French. She told everyone how she single-handedly had raised her children after his death and they all became doctors and lawyers and pilots and famous composers. Then she started telling them how the twenty-four-year-old civil war divided her family up, and brothers fought brothers over some stupid ideological notions that proved terribly bloody yet pointless afterwards. Then she told them about our journey across the Pacific Ocean in this crowded fishing boat where thirst and starvation nearly did us all in until it was her idea to eat some of the dead and drink their blood so that the rest of us could survive to catch glimpses of this beautiful America and become Americans.

Grandma told them too about the fate of Vietnamese women who must marry and see their husbands and sons go to war and never come back. Then she recited poems and told fairy tales with sad endings, fairy tales she herself had learned as a child, the kind she used to tell me and Nancy and my cousins when we were real young. There was this princess, you see, who fell in love with a fisherman, and he didn't know about her 'cause she only heard his beautiful voice singing from a distance. So when he drifted down-river one day, she fell sick and died, her heart turned into this ruby with the image of his boat and his silhouette imprinted on it. There was also this faithful wife who held her baby, waiting for

her war-faring husband every night on a cliff and, out of pity, the gods turned her
and her child into stone. In Grandma's stories, the husbands and fishermen sometimes come home, but they come home always too late.

Grandma's voice was sad and seductive and words came pouring out of her
like rain and the whole place turned quiet and Nancy sobbed 'cause she understood and Eric stood close to me and I cried a little, too.

"I lost four of my children," Grandma said, "twelve of my grandchildren,
and countless relatives and friends to wars and famines and I lost everything I
owned when I left my beautiful country behind. Mine is a story of suffering and
sorrow, suffering and sorrow being the way of Vietnamese life. But now I have a
second chance and I am not who I was, and yet I have all these memories, so
wherever I go, I figure I'll keep telling my stories and songs."

Applause broke out then and afterwards this rich-looking man with gray hair
and in a pinstripe suit came up to Grandma and they talked quietly for a while.
When they were done Grandma came to me and Nancy and Eric to say good-bye.
She said she was not going to wait for my parents to come home for a traditional
funeral. She had a lot of living still to do since Buddha had given her the gift to
live twice in one life and this man, some famous novelist from Colombia, was
going to take her places. He might even help her write her book. So she was going
to the Mediterranean to get a tan and to Venice to see the festivals and ride the
gondolas and maybe afterward she'd go by Hanoi and see what they'd done to
her childhood home and visit some long-forgotten ancestral graves and relatives
and then who knows where she'd go after that. She'd send postcards though and
don't you wait up. Then before we knew it Grandma was already out of the door
with the famous novelist from Colombia and the music started up again and everyone felt pretty good. They hugged each other and there was this feeling in the air,
an enchantment, and if those ice sculptures of ducks and fat little angels with
bows and arrows started to come alive and fly away or something, I swear,
nobody would have been surprised. Eric and I ran out after Grandma after we got
through the hugging frenzy but there was only this city under a velvety night sky,
its high-rises shining like glass cages, with little diamonds and gold coins kept
locked inside them.

Mama and Papa came home two days later. They brought incense sticks and oxhide drums and wooden fish and copper gongs and jasmine wreaths and Oolong tea and paper offerings, all the things that we were supposed to have for a traditional funeral. A monk had even sent a fax for his chanting rate and schedule 'cause he was really busy, and the relatives started pouring in.

It was hard to explain then what had happened, what we had always expected as the tragic ending of things, human frailty, the point of mourning and grief. And wasn't epic loss what made us tell our stories? It was difficult for me to mourn now, though. Difficult 'cause while the incense smoke drifted all over the mansion and the crying and wailing resounded like cicadas humming on the tamarind tree in the summer back in Vietnam, Grandma wasn't around. Grandma had done away with the easy plot for tragedy, and life after her wasn't going to be so simple anymore.

Sister Play

Lan Duong

Sometimes we slept together
because there were not enough beds.
Our legs were like father's pliers
when he tried to play the handyman;
They would lock
together at night, tight and unrelenting.
Our legs, hard and muscular, because we took
after our stout mother,
the shapely calves reminding us
where we came from, that we inherited more than just
pimply backs and an ironic fear of men,
but that we could endure and endure
for a long time after that too.
We used each other as levers to breathe,
and we held on because we had to. Like
the time we played on the slide
and the brown bark on the ground was "FIRE!"

We tried to keep from sliding down, hanging on
to one another, with fingers not yet
painted with the brush of puberty.
Sister 3 on top (because she was older and taller)
and "HOLD ON!" then laughter.
Our bits of legs struggling against
the smooth evil of aluminum.
And sweet-smelling, child-sweat making it slicker
and "FIRE!" was all around.
We played until the slide was no longer hot,
but cool and indifferent.
We left the playground with the brown of bark
on our elbows and we slept that night,
our fingers laced, our strong legs
hurting a little from our play, muscled the other
and we lay entwined,
stronger than an umbilical cord.

Night Shelter

Nguyen Qui Duc

I am running. Three feet off the ground, and in slow motion. Real slow. One step, then another, knees drawn high, straight out in front of me, then dropping down, the feet uncertain, pedaling like a blind man and looking for solid ground maybe. I want my feet to move faster. But it doesn't happen. I keep taking steps and I'm barely moving forward, and that's when I hear Carol.

Carol's a light sleeper. Slightest sound and she's awake. Me, I don't sleep too well either, or too often. When I do, I get these damn dreams, used to frighten Carol so. She's gotten kind of used to them now.

What is it, she asks. She repeats herself in the dark of our bedroom, and I hear her this time. I feel her hand on my hair. My eyes are open now.

Go back to sleep, Carol says. Just go back to sleep. Carol pulls her hand away, moving slightly under the cover.

I am on my back, and I give a grunt. Then I say, sorry, sweet honey, and I lie still, then I hear Carol. She's sighing. Half a yawn, really. I hear her lift her head, and she pulls the pillow straight under her. She's on her side now, facing the window.

You sleep, I say, my eyes rolling sideways toward my wife. Carol doesn't say anything; after a while I hear her breathing, regular now. I sigh, and I close my eyes. Fragments from the dream come back to my mind's eye. The dark mountains, and the fields, and boots. I open my eyes. Carol, I say, a whisper lost in the dark. Carol, I say a bit louder this time. Was I saying something? Did you hear me say something?

My wife doesn't answer. I wait a bit to see if she's heard me, but she's just breathing regularly, like I haven't said anything. I turn on my side, and keep my eyes open, and after a while I start to make out the shapes of the things on the nightstand, wedged between the wall and our bed. I turn and I'm again on my back, I'm hot under the cover and almost sweating. Maybe I am sweating. Carol makes a noise like she's clearing her throat, but it comes out her nostrils. Then she says, I can't sleep. I sigh, and before I say I'm sorry, she says, I don't know what you were saying. You always talk in Vietnamese in your sleep.

I lift the cover and slowly get out of bed. I go to the bathroom for a piss, and out to the back porch for a smoke. It's cold, and dark outside, and quiet, except for the drone of the rain, very light.

I am sitting in our old rattan chair and I have a thin blanket draped over my shoulders and around my upper arms like a poncho. I am holding on to its corners with my left hand, and I have a cigarette in my hand too. With my other hand, I pour myself a bit of brandy from the bottle tucked between the books and the magazines on the shelf underneath the window. After a while it gets warmer, but my feet are cold, and I tuck them under my leg and the blanket gets undone. I have trouble holding both the blanket and the cigarette. I pull one last drag and stand up. I down the brandy and put the cigarette out in the snifter. Then I go inside with the blanket, and the cigarette butt goes in the trash can and the snifter in the sink, and I fall asleep on the sofa.

It's morning and the cat meows like crazy so I get up to feed her. I open a can of wet food for her, and the cat rubs herself against both of my legs. I start to think how it's kind of funny that I talk to my wife in one language, and I dream in another. I go to stand at the kitchen window, and outside, the leaves on the ground are all looking damp, but it has stopped raining. I make myself coffee and listen for sounds from the bathroom. I have a cup of tea ready for Carol when she comes out. I set it on the dining table, and Carol's doing her lips with a small mirror in her hand.

You okay, I ask, and Carol says, yeah, I'm okay. Why?

I was just asking, I say. I go into the kitchen to pour myself some more coffee.

You're not going to forget about Bonzo today, are you, my wife asks as I am about to step out onto the porch.

No, I won't, I call out.

The appointment's at eleven, and it's the new vet down by the hardware store. She hates that other place.

She's just a cat, I say when I come back to the dining room. Cats hate vets.

I'll take her then. I'll take her tomorrow evening or something, if you don't want to take her.

I didn't say I wouldn't take her, I say.

You hate to go anywhere. Except at night. You're lying next to me, and you're gone halfway across the world.

Carol and I both suck in a deep breath, and I go back into the kitchen. Let me know when you're ready, I say and head for the back porch to smoke a cigarette. When I get there, I reach for the brandy from the bookshelf, and I pour a bit of it in my coffee. I put the bottle away, but just before I set it down, I pull it back out again and decide I could pour some more in my coffee. And I do. Bonzo comes charging out of the kitchen in one of her crazy morning runs. She startles me a little, and I pour some of the brandy on the rug. Bonzo, I say, you and me, we're going to the vet today. You'd better be ready at ten thirty, ten forty-five, latest. Or you're in deep doodoo with me and Mama. Meow, meow, I say when the cat doesn't answer.

Bonzo sticks her nose where the brandy is for just a second, then she pauses and looks at me, her body in that weird pose cats get into, head low to the ground, front paws gathered together, her ass and her tail sticking way up in the air. She twitches her nose, and I make like I'm going for her, and real quick, she jumps and zips back into the kitchen, pushing the screen door open with her face. It swings back and slaps the door frame with a loud noise just as Carol calls out to me. I go in and grab the keys to our car and prepare to take Carol to her job downtown. That damn cat, she says. Always banging that screen door.

I don't know why, but I say, that was me, sweet honey. I banged it. Then I think, maybe when I'm down at the vet, maybe I should go to the hardware store and get me something to keep that door from banging so loudly.

There's this van, skidded onto the pavement over on Stonecreek Way, right in front of the library, and it must have side-swiped the Japanese sedan. We're stuck in the traffic and there's a crowd, and Carol's saying, look at all those cops standing around, waving their arms, for no use.

They're getting witness reports, I say. Like on the TV shows, Tuesday and Thursday afternoons.

Why don't they move everybody out of the way? Reports, for Christ's sake.

I've got to get to work. I'll never make it on time. Shit.

It's just folks not knowing how to drive in the rain, I say.

It isn't raining, Carol says.

I'm about to say, sure you'll make it, we'll get there on time, but Carol's changing the subject. She's talking about Bonzo. She says, have you noticed how the cat's acting kind of weird lately?

Weird how?

She's kind of jumpy is all.

They're all like that. We had five cats in Viet Nam. Jumping all over the place, I'm telling you.

Sure, but that was there, Carol says.

For Christ's sake. Why can't you think, Carol? Cats don't fight in wars, Carol.

Yeah, well, who knows what the hell happened.

I don't say anything. I don't know what to say when Carol comes up with things like that. I know what the hell happened, but I can't explain it. I haven't been able to explain it all these years, why should I now? So, like I said, I don't say anything. We drive past the accident, and I just keep my eyes on the road, and at a few crossroads I see the lights aren't working, and I suppose it's because of the storm over the weekend. I'm crossing Stockbridge, getting ready for the right turn on West Mulberry Drive when Carol starts in on the dream.

She goes, so what was your dream all about last night?

I roll down the window on the driver's side a little, and it blows through and unsettles Carol's hair. Sometimes her hair reminds me so much of the rice fields back home, golden and rich and blowing in the wind.

I mean, did you dream about the soldiers chasing you all over again, Carol asks me. Enemy soldiers chasing you and you can't run, right? Slo-mo, right?

I turn to her a little, and I say, if you know so much about my dreams already, why should I tell you anything?

Yeah, but you're always talking in Vietnamese.

I can't help it that I talk in Vietnamese in my dreams, I say.

Carol's emphasizing each of her words now. But I mean, are you talking to enemy soldiers or something? You're talking to your enemies, right?

I kind of shake my head. And I think of how I've never told Carol everything about the dreams. I mean, it's not that I talk to the enemies in my sleep or anything. It isn't it, wasn't like it was the enemies actually chasing me, really. Sure they're there in my dreams, and they're there when it happened for real back then. But, like I said, I've never told Carol the real thing about it.

Do you dream about anything else, Carol asks as I come over the bridge. Do you ever dream about me?

We're approaching her school now, and I still am not saying anything. I am in fact thinking about Bonzo.

So, are you going to talk to me, Carol says. Are you ever going to talk to me, Carol says. Are you ever going to talk to anyone about what happened back then? For God's sake, Ben. Ben's my American name. It was Carol who gave it to me on account of my Vietnamese name being Binh, meaning peace. That was a month or so after we'd met.

You've got to talk to someone, Carol's saying now.

There isn't anything to talk about, I say. But I've said that before many times, and she doesn't ever believe me.

I hate it when you dream like that, Carol says. You either stop or you do something about it, Ben.

I turn on to Kingspark, and wonder how Bonzo would do in a fight.

Ben, Carol says, you're not answering me. I'm talking to you.

I know, I say. I'm thinking. And true, I am thinking, but I'm still thinking about Bonzo. Ferocious when it comes to food, but not much otherwise, I don't think. Damn cat. I wonder what makes some cats fight and what makes others run away.

I turn into the parking lot and pull over to the side of the building where I usually drop Carol off. You're all right, I say to Carol. You're on time.

Carol sits still for a moment. Then she undoes the seat belt, picks up her purse and her books and holds them in front of her stomach, like she does usually, getting ready to get out of the car. But she doesn't lean over to kiss me. I bend over, and she says my name. She says, Ben, you remember.

Remember what, I say, and lean back.

That's where we met. Right over there, in that classroom. She points to a window on the side of the building. It's painted gray, and the wall is concrete and unpainted. The whole place is gray.

That's true, I say to Carol. That's where we met. Carol was teaching and I was getting this job, and they made me help her teach. I was her assistant, and all the students were Vietnamese refugees, like me. That was a year after I came to America. Now it's been eleven years. And Carol and I, we've been married for eight years. I am thinking, eight years, and that's when Carol's thinking the same thing. She says, you realize we've been married for eight years now, Ben.

Yeah, I say. Eight years, sweet honey.

I hate that, Carol says. I hate it when you call me sweet honey. It's such a weird thing to call somebody sweet honey.

I wait for her to say something else. She looks out the window for a moment, and when she talks, it's like she's talking to herself. I can barely hear her.

She says, the last time I brought up having a child, you went and brought home a cat.

I jump. That's not true, Carol. I gave Bonzo to you for your birthday. It was your birthday gift. Why are you saying this?

Ben, Carol says. Do you sometimes wish you'd married someone else?

I look at Carol, and she looks into my eyes, and she says again, do you? Do you wish sometimes you'd married someone else?

Like who, I say. That's a silly question to ask.

Like a Vietnamese woman, she says.

I shift my gaze, and I turn off the ignition key. What are you saying, I ask, and Carol just sits there.

I say to her, don't be crazy. But I'm thinking, maybe. Maybe if I were with a Vietnamese woman, she would understand. She'd understand my running away from the night shelter that time. She'd know it was the guys from my own unit chasing me, on account of me not staying there, not helping the kid beneath the sandbags. But she'd understand. The enemies were chasing us, and the guys from my own unit were wanting my skin too. I'm thinking all this, but I say to Carol, you're crazy. You're my wife, that's that. There isn't going to be any Vietnamese woman or anyone else. No one, you understand? You should go in, you'll be late.

Carol turns to open the car door. I love you, Ben, she says, real softly. I don't want you to be married to someone else. Go on home now. We'll talk about this later. I'm not crazy. Carol steps out of the car, and I hear her say, you're driving me crazy.

I put out my arm to reach for her, but the door slams on me. Carol, I call out when I open the door on my side and step out. The car's between us now, and we're just standing there, looking at each other.

I've got to run, Ben, she says finally. And then she says, don't forget about Bonzo. See you tonight, she says and walks away.

She's walking fast. No slo-mo. She walks fast and away and just leaves me standing there.

I get back inside, turn the key and give the engine some gas. I say, see you, and then I say, Bonzo. I won't forget Bonzo. I'm not going to forget about Bonzo. I'm not forgetting, I say to myself and slam the door shut.

The Long Biên Bridge

Mộng Lan

Seeing the Long Biên Bridge

on the pastel

map of Hanoi   its image

one-dimensional and slumberous   an undug

grave

I would never have guessed

it for what it really is: a patchwork of engravings

love-entwined names (the skin   easy as words

the unstripping   instants of flesh)

graffiti   mostly *"Cẩm Đái!* No Urinating!"

altered

from bombings shell-shocked   doctored countless times

was it the architect Eiffel

who drew this bridge into reality?

its broad black strokes hanging over the sky

like a leg of the Eiffel Tower

placed across two shores

(2)

the Red River
stripping silt   shale
over crimson shores   fluxes
          urgent   snail-patient   penitent

          the rains
bloat it white and phantasmic
                              at its banks
          she launders the family clothes
next to where the buffalo shits
                         where her children shit
          her swollen ankles   the rings

          the children play mindlessly in satellite
soil loaded with strange
          luster
                    that body of dazzling light

(3)

she's learnt how to talk back
$\qquad\qquad$ without talking
she's learnt how to defend herself
$\qquad$ in her small way

$\qquad\qquad$ her older sister
$\qquad$ who refuses to marry him
sits near the bridge amassing
$\qquad\qquad$ the vegetables for sale
$\qquad$ mounds of mint
$\qquad\qquad$ hills of water spinach
guavas $\quad$ bananas "the poor man's fruit"
$\qquad$ swords of sugarcane
flopping scales like huge tongues
$\qquad\qquad$ ready to weigh

$\qquad\qquad$ discreet as pickpockets
$\qquad\qquad\qquad$ peril waits
between rusty spokes
$\qquad\qquad\qquad$ underneath
$\qquad$ spinning bike tires $\qquad$ but

motion saves the day

(4)

       not having to think
    of motion
the villagers commuting from the countryside
      to the city pedal
no thought but to force the legs   the foot
      on the pedal
the hands from swerving too much
    towards one direction
      the head straight
not really looking at anything   yet at everything

in sync with everybody else
    they know not to hold their breaths

    the wind moves through you in conditional
tense of spokes   tattered clothes
    of conical straw hats battling the physics of movement
      friction between atmospheres
    flapping clothes hinting the body's
        bony outline
hair that knows itself only through the wind

(5)

on this foot-bicycle bridge

the contour of rain and urine
                              stains on bridge columns
arc acidic   motionless

        you who pedal across the bridge
assert a blind
                        urgency akin to sustained
voices
        haunted history

the bridge shudders from the history
                              it remembers

(6)

       rustic bodies
with the weight of the day's work
           splayed over trailing shadows

       bodies illuminated like autumnal
earth   fervent thought

pealing from one outline to another
        the endless chase

in ariel notice
          encaged chickens
    whizz by   chicken feathers
strip the sky of wait
       and water   water

       you know not to hold your breath
    wind-intoxicated
waiting for it
    the minute it comes   you want to escape it
the bridge's light

Golden Gate

Mộng Lan

The logic of nonbeing invades
    the Golden Gate Bridge
  I watch the wind's moods and resolutions
wanting night erasing the lines
      that grow from my body
   to engrave around it
have that as a dish
   something I could eat

   Your fully fed body thrashing
         in the Atlantic waves
was found near the Golden Gate Bridge
     no one understands

   the un-life   the mis-life
drove you to it
   had you known that
     the best thing in the world to be
is struggling

Your body was found
   at the bridge's swollen ankles

(2)

there are few bicyclists here
the ones who brave
the adamant wind are
helmeted professionals or stern amateurs

cars dominate & swerve unflinchingly over the
earth's contours

I pull up your body
breathe my breath into you
and we walk here as far
West as the continent allows
city of existences woven
into one tapestry
brine of sense
brine of space
seething pasts and futures

(3)

Magritte rocks
     shrouded in fog

the rough hewn hands   rose tinctured
     skin bared to much sunlight
          pavement under feet
gravelward runs to sea
     ruffling sea   a flag worn white
          above the bridge of red
rust   looming large
          as the universe
     metal cords thicker than wrists pass us
lax   or hastily as the years
          yet yearly repainted

(4)

tourists eyes gape
at the structure bellowing mythic
in its red rust and fog

suspension of cold breaths
hands of icy fumes
a rock   two rocks overlapping in the mist

a house down below enraptured
in foam and waves
its foundation   red walls and lined roof
a fallen hermetic hand

inconsequential
beneath the bridge
overwhelming as the cosmos

(5)

       dust framed in the body's image
eyes blown truant
           with hair yet are motionless

       city of paved feet stumbling onto gravel
gravel seaward runs
        it is the mind projecting us forward
            the body
holding us back

(6)

the cold wind scatters
our voices toward the impenetrable rocks

then a door appears   door of a tomb

stoic   a metal door bounded by stone
time-occluded
door that would suffer unopened
on the bridge that suspends

the idea
of the person who walks
on it   tardy in apprehension
that suspends

instants of nonbeing

Prints

Christian Langworthy

The day was brisk and windy, the thunderheads
rolled wet leaves over the city, leaves
pressed onto the blackened streets like Japanese prints.
The fresh scent of a new rain hangs in the air.
I am thinking of you. Must be thinking of you.
Thoughts of you come only like this.
Why does autumn undress the way you do?

Yesterday, I thought of black umbrellas.
I had read Max Jacob's
"Black Umbrellas" a few weeks back,
so perhaps that was why, the bodies like mushroom stems—
rigid, damp, and cold, coping with the heavy rain
as best they could, each tethered
to the cold wet streets.

Today, the wet streets are smudged with the colors
of passing cars and buses
and shining headlights. I am thinking of you.
The way you are in my head is like a painting
speaking to a stranger years later.
The city hums with life, a city of elevated
trains, wires, and fire escapes waiting
for someone's misfortune.
Brown, wet leaves lay flattened
against the black, slick streets. I think of the Japanese
prints we saw together at the Institute
and of a haiku by Basho.

Western Music

by Linh Dinh

Outside the glass door of Fish and Chick, the white noise of the motorcycle traffic sputtered: putt, putt, putt, putt. Inside, Skinny and Dercum sat at the bar, their sweat cooled by the air conditioning. Kurt Cobain was screaming on the stereo. It was the beginning of the summer, just before the monsoon season. Skinny was drunk on Jagermeister. He shouted: "I'm sick of this place!"

"So am I!" Dercum said.

"I've got to get out of here."

"We can go have a beer at M.I.G. or Bar Nixon if you like."

"No! No! No! No! What I mean is: I'm sick of Hanoi!"

"Do you want to go back to New York?"

"I don't want to go home. I just need to get away from Hanoi."

"We can go to Sapa."

"No, not Sapa." Skinny took a drag on his Perfume River cigarette. He jabbed his face over his shoulder towards the Israelis, Dutch, Germans, Aussies and Frenchmen sitting at tables behind them. "I'm tired of looking at these Eurotrash!"

"I'll talk to Mai tomorrow."

For $5 a day, Mr. Mai waited every day for Dercum outside the Victory Hotel to take him where he wanted to go. He was Dercum's personal cyclo driver. Wiry, with a bronze complexion, he was in his mid-fifties, a grandfather. He was too well-dressed for his profession. In public he wore a tailored shirt, tie, polyester slacks and imitation leather wing tips. Unlike most men his age, he was not a veteran. He was not allowed to serve because his parents were branded reactionaries by the Viet Minh, who executed his father in 1955 during the Land Reform Program. His mother committed suicide soon after.

Dercum walked out of the hotel lobby and found him, as usual, lounging in his cab beneath the flame tree: "Chao Ong!"

Mr. Mai roused himself from his seat: "How are you doing this morning, Dirt? Where we going?"

"I don't know yet. Maybe nowhere."

"Nowhere very good. I sit here and drink beer." Mr. Mai eased back down, lifted a plastic cup of beer to his lips. His eyes were bloodshot.

Dercum lit a Marlboro: "My friend is getting sick of Hanoi."

"Skin Knee sick of Hanoi?"

"Yes, Skinny is very sick of this place."

"Tell him to go home."

"But he does not want to go home yet."

"Tell him to go to Hanoi Hilton."

"Now, now, let's not get personal. Skinny is sick of looking at the Eu-ro-trash."

"Year-old trash?"

"Eu-ro-trash. Like White Trash," Dercum smiled good-naturedly, "like me, but Eu-ro-pean."

Mr. Mai finished his beer, burped, crossed his leg.

Dercum continued: "We want to go the countryside, somewhere where there's no Europeans or Americans."

Mr. Mai jiggled his empty cup: "For how long, Boss?"

"A week."

"To do what?"

"Do nothing. We just want to relax in the countryside."

Mr. Mai jiggled his cup, thought for a moment, then said: "We can go to my wife's home village."

"Where's that?"

"Three hundred kilometers from Hanoi."

"Nine hours by car?"

"Ten."

"Which direction?"

"West."

"In the mountain?"

"Yes."

"Near Son La?"

"Between Son La and Yen Chau."

"Is there a hotel there?"

"Hotel?!"

Dercum called Skinny at the Metropole: "It's all arranged. We're going to the sticks for a week."

"Sounds excellent."

"You should bring along cans of SPAM as a precaution."

"Don't worry. I've eaten ox penises and dogs."

"You have?"

"And sparrows."

"What else have you eaten?"

"Wouldn't you like to know."

"And we should bring along seven cases of beer. A case for each day."

"I'm really looking forward to this."

"I'll bring the toilet paper."

Dercum Sanders and Skinny, whose real name was Dave Levy, had met at Columbia. Dercum never finished college but dropped out after his sophomore year. First he worked as a bike messenger, then as a sous-chef at Coute Que Coute in midtown, then as a luggage handler for United Airlines, which allowed him to travel to Asia for free, and then his grandmother died... Before Dercum left New York, he said he was going to Vietnam to teach English, but after his first week in Hanoi, he thought, "Why should I feel apologetic about not working? Why shouldn't I just hang out?" After six months in Vietnam, he sent a fax to Skinny: "You must come over soon. This place is wild. COMPLETE FREEDOM. One feels uninhibited here. I feel like a new man. I am a new man. I cannot wait to see your face again. I think about you day and night. I mean it. In New York nothing is possible. Now I see my past in a new light. You must come over."

It took Mr. Mai three days to make arrangements for the trip. Dercum and Skinny would split the cost of hiring a four wheel drive, at $600 a week, gas and driver included. The party would be comprised of Dercum, Skinny, the driver and Mr. Mai.

To avoid traffic, they decided to leave first thing in the morning. The car showed up promptly at 5 AM in front of the Victory Hotel. It was a Jeep Cherokee. They started loading. Dercum said to Mr. Mai: "All this beer is for you."

Mr. Mai stared at the cases of Heineken filling the luggage compartment and shook his head convulsively: "Not enough!"

"Not enough?!" Dercum shouted with feigned astonishment. Everyone laughed except the driver, a burly, bearded man in jeans and a pale blue T-shirt with "MOUNTAIN EVEREST IS THE HIGHEST MOUNTAIN IN THE WORLD" on the front and "SOLO FUCKER" on the back.

"You want a beer now?" Dercum asked Mr. Mai.

"Sure." Dercum handed him a beer. "And one for the driver."

Dercum handed a beer to the driver.

"Thank you, mate!" the driver said.

"Mr. Mai, please tell him that we're not Australians."

"They're not Australians."

"I'm Dercum." Dercum shook the driver's hand.

Mr. Mai interjected: "Dirt!"

"It's actually 'Dirk'"

"Dirt," the driver said.

"And this is Skinny."

"Skin Knee."

"What is your name?"

"Long." On closer inspection, Long appeared to be only about 30, although his beard and scowl had made him seem much older.

"Long?"

"Long."

Skinny looked at Dercum with a twinkle in his eyes. "How long?" he blurted. Dercum burst out laughing. Long stared at Mr. Mai, his face blank.

"Never mind," Dercum said.

"I think I want a beer also," Skinny said.

"I didn't know you drink beer at five in the morning," Dercum said as he handed Skinny a Heineken.

"Skin Knee is becoming Vietnamese," Mr. Mai exclaimed.

Dercum and Skinny sat in the back. Mr. Mai sat up front. All except Long were elated as the car started moving. At that hour, the streets were filled with people of all ages: walking, jogging, doing tai chi, kicking a soccer ball or a shuttlecock, or playing badminton. They passed a squadron of legless men rolling briskly down Le Hong Phong Street on wheelchairs. "Old VC," Mr. Mai said. Long tapped a Morse-like staccato on his horn. On the tape deck was Louis Armstrong singing Fats Waller: "What did I do...to be so black and blue?"

"Do you like Louis Armstrong, Mr. Mai?" Dercum asked.

Mr. Mai didn't answer him. He was suddenly withdrawn, reflective, charmed by the sights of his home city. Each scene was made novel from the vantage point of a speeding car.

"I like jazz and blues," Long said.

Most of the motor traffic they encountered was going the other way: people coming into the city from outlying villages. Within twenty minutes, the houses thinned out on both sides. Long tapped on his horn constantly, passing motorcycles, bicycles, trucks, buses and cars while dodging chickens, pigs, cows, dogs, men and buffalo. After three hours, the road turned to gravel. Mr. Mai rolled the window down four times to throw up his three cans of beer.

Long said: "Easy, Grandfather."

Mr. Mai moaned: "I'm not used to sitting in a car."

Dercum said: "We should stop for lunch soon, Long."

Long turned his head around: "Good place to eat: twenty minutes." The car ran over a dog. Long could see a rapidly diminishing black shape twitching in the rear view mirror.

"Sounds good."

"Twenty minutes."

"Boys! I think we just ran over a dog!" Skinny yelped.

"Did we just run over a dog, Long?" Dercum asked.

"No."

"Can I have another beer?" Mr. Mai said.

Long drove the Cherokee onto the side of the road. The little eatery was fronted by a pool table beneath fiberglass awning propped up by bamboo poles.

They walked past a glass cabinet displaying imported liquors and cigarettes, stepped over a dozing yellow dog and entered a bright, airy room. On its lime-colored walls were posters of busty white women hugging enormous beer bottles. Up high in one corner was a shelf-altar: In front of a framed, retouched black and white photograph of a handsome, smooth-faced, doe-eyed cadet was a sand-filled teacup holding joss sticks, a plate of mandarin oranges and a plate of boiled chicken. At the back of the room, a very old woman sat, all bunched up and immobile, on a bamboo settee in front of a very large, very loud TV, watching a soap opera. They sat down on little plastic stools at a low table. They were the only patrons. The waitress came out from the kitchen and said: "Today we have fried catfish and wild boar."

Mai ordered: "Bring those dishes, Sister. And fried tofu, boiled watercress, two bowls of soup."

"What nationality are these people, Uncle?"

"American."

"They look like Russians."

"They're gay."

"Gay!"

"Hurry up, Sister, we are all starving to death!"

The waitress went back to the kitchen.

"What did you tell her?" Skinny asked Mai.

"She said you look Russian. I said you are Americans."

Dercum asked: "Where are we?"

"Thao Nguyen."

Long said to Mai: "Are they really gay?"

"Of course!"

A gaggle of giggling children stood outside the restaurant to stare at Skinny and Dercum. Skinny smiled at them and said: "Boo!" The bravest of the children separated himself from the group and, with goading from the rest, shouted in English: "I love you!" before running away. The rest of them scattered, scream-ing: "I love you! I love you!"

Everyone but Skinny sat at the table picking their teeth with toothpicks after the meal. The waitress wiped the table cursorily with a rag, sweeping the little fish bones onto the tiled floor. She was wearing a lurid pink shirt with little black dots and red flowers. On her hair was a bright yellow bow. Long said to her: "Sister, do you want to go the mountain with us?"

"There is nothing but ghosts and savages in those mountains!" She smiled and walked back to the kitchen.

In college, Skinny and Dercum were not lovers. Each refused to acknowledge the unbearable fact of his attraction to the other by frantically trying to become a heterosexual. They dated many women, overlapping on occasions. But they remained emotional intimates, returning to each other for comfort after each failed relationship. When Dercum left for Vietnam, Skinny had just come out. Dercum was still undecided. Their love was consummated in Skinny's suite at the Metropole Hotel a day after his arrival.

The car climbed steadily. The road was mostly bad, alternating between asphalt, dirt and gravel. They passed tea plantations, a litchi forest, fields of maize and fields of tobacco. They drove through Viet towns of wooden and white-washed brick houses; Black Thai *bản* of houses on stilts, with cows and buffalo beneath them; a Kha Mu village of thatch-roofed huts with walls of woven bark. In every Viet town there was at least one cafe with a sign outside advertising "karaoke." They saw a group of Flower Hmongs. One of the men carried a flint-lock rifle. The women had woven horse hair into their own, creating enormous turbans. Neither Skinny nor Dercum said anything for a long time. Long glanced at the rear view mirror: the two men were asleep leaning against each other.

Mr. Mai said: "How long have you been a driver?"

"Just a year."

"It seems like a great job."

"You get to see places."

"And you get to meet foreigners."

Long chuckled: "There are classy foreigners, but there are some who are impossible to deal with."

"Like who?"

"Last week, I drove three Koreans. They were very unfriendly."

"How are the Americans?"

"They're actually not bad. Most of them tip."

"Any women?"

"Huh?"

"You know: you meet any women?"

Long chuckled: "A couple."

Mr. Mai waited for Long to continue. Long continued: "Most of them travel with a husband or a boyfriend. And then you have the old and Christian ones, who travel in pairs, but every now and then, you catch yourself an odd single."

Mr. Mai waited for Long to continue. Long continued: "For example, a couple months ago, I drove three people from New Zealand: a couple and a single girl, all college students. I drove them to Sapa, where we stayed in two rooms at The Auberge. The girl's name was Hillary. She was my girlfriend for a week."

Mr. Mai had a pained look on his face, made an unconscious sucking noise with his throat.

Long chuckled: "I evened the score a little, you know."

"Ah," Mr. Mai sighed, "but I'm an old man and a grandfather."

"And then there was this other one. American. Becky her name was. After I drove her to Halong Bay on a day trip, I would come to her hotel in Hanoi three or four times a week for a month. She was a sex maniac, this Becky was. I'm not your girlfriend, she said, I just want sex. Fine with me, I said. She was sleeping with at least two or three other guys, as far as I could tell. This girl couldn't get enough of it. She was delirious. She asked me, 'Am I pretty?' 'Sure you are,' I told her. And she was pretty. Maybe not that pretty, but pretty. She told me one night, 'I'm a very ugly girl, a very ugly girl.' She was actually crying over this, that's how crazy she was."

"Maybe in America they don't think she's so pretty."

Long furrowed his brows. He wasn't sure whether to become angry.

"You know, it's the same with some of the Vietnamese girls we see hanging on the arms of foreigners. We think these girls are ugly, but the foreigners think they're very pretty. They think some of these girls the most beautiful women on the face of this earth." Mr. Mai glanced at the back seat: "At least these two," he deepened his voice, "are not corrupt!-ing the chaste women of Vietnam with their decadent, imperialistic, materialistic pollution!"

"Ha! ha!"

"Actually, these two guys don't seem to like other white people. They requested that I take them somewhere where there's no Americans."

Long was glad the conservation had veered away from his sex life. What a dirty old man this Mai is, he thought. "But the whole country is crawling with Americans."

"That's true."

"If not live ones, then dead ones."

"That's true."

"How do you know there's no Americans in Muom Village?"

"I've been there three times. It's my wife's native village."

"How did she end up in Hanoi?"

"I kidnapped her!"

"Ha! Ha!"

"Actually, my wife served in the Army. That's how she made it to Hanoi."

"I figured."

"In my family, the decorated veteran is a woman!"

"Ha! Ha!"

"Hey, it worked out great for me: if she was near her family, there was no way they would have let her marry me."

"And how do they treat you now?"

"Like shit!"

"Ha! Ha!"

"Stop for a second."

Long stopped the car to let Mr. Mai out. Dercum opened his eyes, saw the back of Long's head, forgot where he was, panicked, recovered, closed his eyes again. Long thought: What a concept: gay Americans!!! But they all seem so... so...so...thick! So macho! All body hair and meat and sweat and swagger. Well, maybe not the Skin Knee guy.... Were gays allowed in the US Army? Can there be such a thing as a gay imperialist? Mr. Mai climbed back in: "I feel much better."

After they started moving again, Mr. Mai said: "You know, Brother, there's an American ghost in Muom Village."

"Really?"

"My wife said that, in '69, a plane was shot down over Muom Village, and they found the pilot's leg in the forest."

"Just his leg?"

"Yes, but it was a very big leg. My wife told me it was as tall as a man's chest. This guy was a giant."

"They're all giants."

"But this guy was really a giant."

"People tend to be shorter in the mountains anyway."

"It's the lack of nutrients."

"No sodium."

"That's right. The villagers buried this leg where they found it, but his ghost began to show up at night, knocking on people's doors and asking for water."

Long took a sip from his Heineken: "Why do ghosts ask for water anyway?"

"Not all ghosts. Only the ones who have lost a lot of blood while dying."

"And did his entire body show up, or just his leg?"

"What do you mean?"

"When he knocked on people's doors at night, what did people see: a leg, or the entire body?"

"You really don't know?"

"No, I don't."

Mr. Mai raised his voice: "When you die, it doesn't matter if all that's left of you is your asshole, you come back as a whole person."

"I didn't know that."

"That's because you grew up in the city."

"You're right. There are no ghosts in the city."

"There are a few, but not many. There are not many ghosts in the city because of electricity."

"Tell me more about the American ghost."

"This guy kept bothering the villagers, always showing up at night and asking for water, so they went back to the burial site and erected a little shrine. After that, he stopped bothering them."

"He's getting more than he deserves for dropping bombs on them," Long chuckled.

"But you can't hold a grudge against a dead man. I've seen this shrine: There was a bottle of wine and a cassette player."

"A cassette player?"

"Yes, a cassette player playing Soviet music."

"Why Soviet music?"

"Because they didn't have tapes of American music. This was in 1989, in a place where 'monkeys cough, herons crow,' where 'dogs eat rocks, chickens eat pebbles!'"

"Whose idea was it to play him music?"

"I don't know. But it makes sense if you think about it. They probably thought that since he was so far away from home, he would appreciate hearing some Western music."

Dercum made a little noise. Without opening his eyes, he said: "Are we almost there, Mr. Mai?"

"We're almost there."

"The only Americans I want to see this week are these two guys back there," Long said. "I don't want to see any ghost."

"Don't worry."

But Mr. Mai did not explain to Long why the American ghost could not go home again. Maybe it was because he did not know the reason himself—he is, after all, also a city person.

When the American pilot was shot out of the sky, his body was scattered across several bodies of water. And a ghost, as any peasant will tell you, cannot cross a body of water, even a tiny brook, unless his own body is whole. So this American had nowhere to go but to stay where he was. From that point on, Muom Village would have to become his village. His asking for water from the villagers was only a ruse to be allowed inside someone's house. That is, until they decided to build him his own house: the shrine. What the peasants saw when they opened their door to the American was simply his wish to be whole again. They all noticed, for example, that his uniform was untorn, and unstained by blood.

They crossed a truss bridge spanning a deep, leafy ravine, then turned onto a twisting dirt road descending steeply into a narrow valley. Crowding the road on both sides were elephant grass, patches of daisies, mango trees, mangosteens, bamboo, creepers and a hundred different vines even the locals don't have names for. A copper-colored river appeared and disappeared through the foliage. Shafts of pale light pierced through the bluish gray clouds and in the sky, someone's kite was spiraling. Now they saw the first villager: a small girl walking towards them alongside an albino buffalo. As they passed, she stared at them blankly and did not wave. Now came the village: thirty houses clustered together, surrounded by rice paddies. The encircling mountains were covered by mist.

Auspicious

Bich Minh Nguyen

My father has been studying every room in the house
before he remodels. He wakes up early to survey
the light, walks around taking notes as if he hasn't lived here for years.
His sketchbook is filled with plans, drawings, and, in the back,
words he's learned: *valance, voile,* and the word he asks me to explain,
auspicious. Every word is an empty house in this morning.
He waits for dense heat, impeccable brilliance, for the sky
to be what it was when he was growing up in Vietnam, the sky
hazy, heavy. In the dining room he is writing *auspicious:*
a good sign; a bright morning. He says, *Just imagine the sunrise*
through these dining room windows. Crimson valances
offset by white voile! For even in the darker shades of red
there exists a brightness. And it is this memory,
this desire to see original color, that brings him here,
measuring the morning, looking out in order to see inside
the room. Thirty years ago, in Vietnam, he painted water scenes.
He traveled to the beaches of Nha Trang
and painted in the dark, shading in the whites and yellows
to create a disappearing day. But afterwards
he couldn't find the morning in the nights of canvas,
couldn't find where it was he had tried to begin.

Placing the Accents

Truong Tran

left undisturbed on the piano's mantel
ashes of incense in a cup of sand
ikebana flowers leaning towards morning
left to die on a converted shrine
a deserted home lived in only
by the presence of your portrait

*

lão già—old man come sit down and drink some tea
I've brewed oolong your favorite
as a child I watched you unraveling
tea leaves still wet and warm
in your palm we found butterflies   frogs
an elephant with two ears   a trunk   a tail
imagine finding an elephant
in the belly of a teapot

*

she left not long ago
with suitcase   car keys   a fold-up mattress
to act a stranger in a stranger's home
some white rice in a bowl
a few slivers of bitter melon
pickled and placed in a saucer of fish sauce
this is all that she will have
she says eating bitter is what she does best

*

it was the first real conversation
we had in months

hoa fuchsias của Bố
dã chết chưa

not yet Ma,
dying but not dead.
when are you coming...

Shhh...

                                                  *

she helped me write this poem
with eyeglasses tilted on the bridge of her nose
pen in hand as if holding a needle
she embroidered the accents onto this paper cloth
as you would have done with chisel   hammer
your voice demanding   *It's time you learn*

Mango

Christian Langworthy

My brother and I were the sons of my mother's clients. She never told us their names. She just said that they were both killed in the war. One father died in a helicopter accident, the other was ambushed while crossing a bridge. She told the same story to all of our neighbors, but even as a child, I sensed that she was lying. She never cried when she related these stories to anyone and seemed to enjoy each moment of the retelling. She even laughed once, recounting to a woman how she loved my brother's father more than she loved mine.

My mother's clients were all around us, on the street corners and in the pool halls. They were prison guards, truck drivers, mechanics and pilots. They were sergeants and majors, captains and corporals. My brother and I watched as they performed their military duties in the prisons, on the streets, or on the landing zones. We watched them pilot their Hueys and Chinooks, and caught bubble gum thrown from the back of deuce-and-a-halfs. They were our heroes, and we were fascinated by their weapons of war. We often imitated the way they walked and carried their rifles. We played war games on the streets with the neighborhood boys. Every military piece of trash that we found became a prized possession: belt buckles, brass shells, helmet liners, or canteens. But the most prized items were live rounds. We spent endless hours trying to fire the rounds, striking the priming caps with nails or dropping them off rooftops onto cement. We unscrewed the bullets from their brass casings and used the black powder to make crude firecrackers which we threw as if we were throwing grenades. We wanted to be soldiers. We wanted to march on the streets with the men in the green uniforms. But what my brother and I wanted was for one of these men to be our father though my mother told us our fathers were dead.

My mother's clients talked to us in a language we didn't understand. They patted our shoulders, handed us candy, and the men who stayed for more than a day bought us toys like boxing gloves and battery-powered toy jets. We never saw our mother sleeping with these men. She would leave for a day and come back late at night, and if she was with a client, we always heard whispers and hushed voices.

One afternoon though, during the height of the monsoon season, my brother and I slept in the far back of the bungalow behind a make-shift bamboo partition. It was dark in the bungalow and we awoke suddenly disturbed. Through the pattering of the monsoon rain, we heard voices groaning. Being curious, we both went out to the front room, which was lit by a hurricane lamp. In the center of the room on a table, an American man was on top of our mother. My brother and I, our curiosities piqued, approached the table and walked around it. Our mother told us to go back to sleep, but we ignored her and watched. She was wearing a blouse, but was naked from the waist down, and the man's green trousers hung around his ankles. His hips moved up and down and his penis was inside our mother. He said something and our mother yelled at us, and we ran into the far back room where we always pretended to be asleep. Lying on floor mats, we heard the man yell at our mother and the door slam shut as he left.

Weeks passed, the monsoon season ended, and the men in the green uniforms entered and left our lives. More and more often, they were sleeping in our bungalow. One man let my brother and me drink a little whiskey after he had sex with our mother. Another man was taken away by M.P.'s who knocked on our door in the middle of the night. Whenever we could, we slept cuddled with our mother, but her clients took most of her nights. It was only during the afternoons, when temperatures were too hot to do anything, that our mother napped with us in the cool air of the bungalow and held us in her arms.

One day, my brother and I returned from playing on the streets to take a nap. A soldier was with our mother. She told us that he was staying for a short while. My stomach felt sick. My brother went into the bungalow and lay down, but I ran back out to the streets. Something had gotten into me. I searched for a stick, a long piece of metal, anything, but all that I could find was an ice-cream stick broken in half lengthwise down the middle. Wielding the ice-cream stick in my hand like a knife, I went back to the bungalow. My mother and the soldier had come out to look for me. I confronted them near a neighbor's clotheslines where white bed sheets hung. "I'll kill you," I shouted at the soldier and waved the ice-cream stick threateningly. "Go away."

He did not understand what I had said, but he understood my body language. He laughed. My mother was furious. She was going to hit me, but the soldier stopped her. He pulled money from his pockets and extended his hand. I grabbed the money and ran to the nearest street vendor where I bought a pop-pistol and roamed the streets, shooting at people until it was time to go home.

2

My mother was angry with me for a few days after I threatened her client, but her anger soon passed. She invited a new neighbor and her son over for an evening tea. The neighbor lived in a tree house close to the alley that led from the dirt road to our bungalow. I watched her climb down a ladder. Her son followed. I looked back up at the tree house, noticing how empty it looked. Rags hung from the windows. A rope tied to a tin pail swayed, slightly disturbed by their climbing. They lived right above a chicken-wire fence shrouded in green by tomato and stink fruit vines which had intertwined.

The two mothers drank tea. I went with my brother and the neighbor's son to play near a ditch filled with broken glass and lined with concertina wire under the walls of the prison. Unlike my brother and me, our neighbor was full-blooded Vietnamese, and he had a tennis ball which we threw back and forth and kicked around. He told us his mother was a seamstress, but that he and his mother were adjusting to life without his father, who had just recently been killed fighting the war against the communists. Now they were living in the tree house to save money so his mother could pay off old debts. As we played with the ball, it got steadily dark and the prison searchlights began making rounds in the night sky above the city. We heard our mothers' calls and were about to go home when our neighbor kicked the tennis ball one last time, catching my brother and me off guard. The ball flew past our feet and rolled into the ditch.

"I'll get it," said the neighbor. "It's my fault it went in the ditch."

My brother and I watched as he walked down into the ditch. He carefully wove his way through some concertina wire, bent over and picked up the tennis ball. As he started to back up out of the wire, he screamed in pain. "What happened?" my brother and I blurted. We both jumped into the ditch.

"I stepped on some glass," he said, crying. "I'm bleeding."

We carried him out of the ditch and took off his sneakers. He was wailing by then. My brother said, "He's not that heavy. Here, you take his sneakers and he can lean on me as we walk back."

"Okay," I said. I took the sneakers from my brother, who then put our neighbor's arm around his shoulder. It struck me that I should put the boy's other arm on my shoulder, but something kept me from doing it. We walked slowly back. The neighbor limped on one foot and leaned on my brother. He cried uncontrollably. He was a mess. I felt useless just carrying the sneakers. One sneaker was a dirty white canvas and the other was stained completely red by the blood. A guard watched us from his tower as we walked back along the length of the prison wall.

When we were in the alley, the neighbor's mother ran to her son. She was in hysterics and kept yelling, "What happened?"

"He stepped on some glass in the ditch," I said. Now it seemed the boy was wailing more and more in front of his mother.

"You took him to the prison ditches?" my mother asked. "Why didn't you play somewhere else?" She saw the boy leaning on my brother's shoulder.

"I don't know," I said.

"We always play there," my brother said. The light in the alley was getting darker. I could not see the tomatoes or the stink fruit on the vines anymore. We went back to the bungalow, which was lit by the hurricane lamp. The boy's mother was upset. "How could you let that happen to my boy?" she mumbled.

"I'm sorry," my mother said, embarrassed. "They should have been more careful." She eyed me as I dropped the sneakers onto the cement floor of the bungalow. They wrapped the boy's foot in some cloths and put his foot up and gave him lemonade. He had stopped crying.

"It was an accident," the boy said as we sat around the tea settings. "Just an accident. I couldn't walk, so Sa helped me."

"Thank you, Sa," the woman said. "Thank you for helping my son. You're a true hero."

My mother glared at me. "Why didn't you help? You didn't help at all," she yelled.

"I carried his sneakers," I said.

"Your friend cuts his foot badly, needs help to walk, and all you can do is carry his sneakers?"

"I didn't really need his help," my brother intervened.

My mother still glared at me. Resentment kept me from defending myself. I was angry at my mother for leaving us all the time, angry with losing her to her clients, and yet I had always wanted to please her so she would not run away from us. I blamed myself for her absences, and it hurt my feelings that she thought badly of me. I had not done anything wrong, and my resentment and hurt kept me silent.

The boy's mother, no longer worried about her son and pleased with my mother's reprimand, broke the silence. "Your boys. Do they know their fathers?"

"No," my mother said. "They both died in the war before the boys were born."

My mother told the story again: the grenade, the bridge, the helicopter. A lump grew in my throat. My chest hurt. I saw my brother holding back his emotions too. The boy's mother saw our discomfort. She said, "Maybe we should stop. Your boys—"

"Oh, they always get like that," my mother said.

"How long did you see each of them?" the woman asked.

"Almost a year each and then, well, they died when I was pregnant, first with Phuong and then Sa."

"It must be a handful, raising two boys by yourself," the woman said. "You must have a favorite."

"Oh, yes. Sa is my favorite," my mother said casually. "I love him more than Phuong. Sa's father was good to me." She laughed and hugged my brother.

My chest felt like it had a big hole in it. I tried to swallow the lump in my throat. I wondered what my father had done to my mother. It was hard enough to hear my mother say that she loved my brother more than she loved me, but it was even harder to learn that my father wasn't good to her. I thought of him as a hero. I thought my mother must have loved him. But her words shattered me. My mother did not love me much, and she did not love my father. I looked down to hide my tears and tapped my fingers on the cement. Down the alley, I saw the huge walls of the prison, the guard towers and the searchlight. My mind was buzzing with images of the ditch, the man with his penis inside my mother, and the ice-cream stick.

"I'm thirsty," my brother said. His voice interrupted my thoughts. My mother poured him a glass of lemonade. She set the pitcher down and looked at me.

"You can't have any lemonade," she said. As the searchlights swept the night sky, I sat in front of my mother and her company and, as the conversation flowed, I pretended that I was not thirsty, that I did not notice the empty glass in front of my feet.

3

When my mother was with her clients, I went in search of her. I looked down streets busy with the traffic of bicycles, rickshaws and cyclos, hoping to catch a glimpse of her. I wanted to see what she did every day and where she went.

I heard her say to a neighbor of ours that she was having an affair with a gentleman down the road, someone who was rich, a foreigner who was married.

"What's an affair?" I asked the neighbor, after my mother had left.

"Oh, so you've been listening," she said. She was washing her clothes by hand in a water trough underneath a persimmon tree. "Well, let me see. An affair is when two people have to meet in secret."

"But why do they meet in secret?" I asked.

"So that no one finds out about it." She wrung the water out of a pair of underwear and slapped them against the side of the trough.

"What happens if someone finds out about it?"

"Then they get in big trouble," she said.

"Why?" I asked.

"Because it's supposed to be a secret." She was almost done washing her clothes. Her laundry basket was full of twisted clumps of wet clothing. "Look, I have to hang up my clothes now."

"Please. Please, just one more question?" I begged her. She stood with her basket balanced against her waist.

"Okay. Just one more and that's it."

"What do they do in secret?" I asked.

She paused for a second, and then she said, "They kiss."

"Oh," I said, not quite understanding the implications, but I knew enough to know that this man was taking my mother away from my brother and me. So I staked out the residence that I thought was his home. It had to be his residence because he had a wall around his house. Only rich people had walls around their houses. I climbed a tree outside the premises and scouted the grounds. His front yard had grass and an apricot tree close to the wall and the tree I had nestled into, and he had two dogs. Days came and went, and I hid every day in the tree branches and watched until he came out and left his residence. I was obsessed with finding out if he was my mother's lover. I saw him leave once wearing a white suit so in my mind he was a rich man. He had to be the man with whom my mother was having an affair. He was a mystery to me, and a child's superstition made me think that he was a ghost. The thought of that white suit was scary to me, and even more so because my mother was spending time with him. I felt compelled to save my mother from becoming a ghost herself. So I watched him. It became my mission. My mother's life depended on it. I scouted him as though he were the enemy. He had a motorbike in his driveway, and in my reconnaissance, I noticed that when he left each day, he put his dogs in the house.

In the days that I had been watching him, I never saw my mother entering or leaving the premises, but I did see the plump apricots hanging from his tree. Each day I saw the apricots, I was hungry. My hunger grew to the point where I could think of nothing but snagging an apricot and biting into it.

When the man in the white suit left one day, I climbed out on a branch and jumped on top of the wall and from there, jumped to the apricot tree. I was proud of my cleverness and rewarded myself with the ripe apricots. The apricots were sweet and succulent, but what I really tasted was the joy of adventure and freedom to do anything I wanted. The city of Da Nang was my playground and as I ate the apricots, it never occurred to me that I was a thief.

But the apricots were not enough to satisfy me. I wanted more. I wanted to impress the neighborhood children. So instead of keeping the apricot tree a secret, I showed it to them. I even convinced myself that I was benevolent though I did it mainly to be accepted by others.

With two other boys, I returned to the apricot tree. The three of us sat in its branches, and as the others feasted on the ripe fruits, I told them the story of the ghost. I told them about my mother and how I would have to rescue her from the clutches of the man in the white suit. Though they listened intently, I still embellished upon the story out of a sense of worthlessness. I reported to them the difficulties of my reconnaissance missions. I altered the stories. Simple events became heightened dramas. Each encounter with my mother's lover was filled with risks and danger. I tried to enlist their help by scaring them. I told them the man in the white suit would turn everyone's mother into a ghost. They ate the apricots with their eyes wide open. But then, in the midst of my tale, I noticed movement somewhere on the lawn. My heart stopped. It was the dogs. They bounded out seemingly from nowhere and circled the tree and barked. They were Dobermans and vicious. "Now, we're trapped," said the older of the two boys.

"I'm not jumping back onto that wall," said the other. "What if I don't make it?" He was right. They were both right. We were all trapped in the tree. We had to wait until the dog's owner came home. "He's going to kill us," said the younger boy. "He'll feed us to his dogs."

An hour or so later, the ghost returned and opened the gate to his residence. There were not many apricots left on his tree. "Help," we cried.

He looked surprised and then angry at our presence, then saw his Dobermans sitting on their haunches, guarding the tree. He said something in a foreign language to them, then walked to his house and opened the front door, whistling to his dogs. They bounded into the house. He closed the door behind them. Then he stared at us from across the yard. We knew he was letting us go, so we scrambled off the tree and ran out the gate onto the street, laughing nervously and running until we ran out of breath.

On the way home, I straggled far behind the other boys who had run ahead to meet their friends. I was disappointed that I had not found my mother. I looked down all the streets and alleys, but she was nowhere to be found. Then I passed by a pool hall and heard the cracking of balls through a screen door. I pressed my face hard against the screen and shielded my eyes from the bright sun. The pool hall was smoky and dark. A man was chalking his cue stick. Soldiers in green uniforms sat along the counter of the bar and swiveled on their bar stools. I wanted to watch the pool players, so I opened the screen door, but before I could take two steps, I heard something directed at me in a foreign language. Then another voice said in Vietnamese, "Get out of here, boy." I stopped mid-step. In a far corner, I saw a black, silk dress with floral prints. I could only see the woman's back, but I saw a man's hands caressing her thighs. I ran out of the pool hall. The soldiers were laughing. I ran home as fast as I could and, to my relief, my mother was back again. She was not wearing a black, silk dress, but she was wearing lipstick and earrings. I knew she had just returned from her work. My brother played with his boxing gloves. Sitting on the patio, my mother watched him jabbing at an invisible opponent. I approached.

"What happened to your face?" my mother asked.

"Nothing," I said.

"Here, look." My mother gave me a small, hand mirror with a pink back. I studied my face. The screen door had left its imprint of lines. My brother started laughing.

"How did you do that?" he asked.

"At the pool hall," I said. "I was looking through a screen door."

"I want you to stay away from there," my mother said. "That's not a place for children."

"I was just watching the pool players," I replied and looked in the mirror again. The lines were fading, and just as I was ready to hand the mirror back to my mother, I saw the reflection of a man in fatigues coming out of the doorway of our bungalow. He said hello in Vietnamese with a bad accent. He was an American soldier with blonde hair and blue eyes. Suddenly, I felt shy. Still carrying the mirror, I walked quickly to the back room. "It's time for their naps anyway," I heard my mother say. I knew she wanted to be alone with the soldier.

My brother and I lay down on our sleeping mats. A large lizard rested on the far wall. Before long, my brother was sleeping. I wondered if the soldier was my father, or maybe my brother's. I held the mirror above my head and tried to see if I had any blonde hairs, but there were none. I set the mirror down and turned over on my back. I heard the rhythms of a helicopter flying over Da Nang. My mother and the American had moved into the front room. They talked in muted voices. Soon, I heard their groans and whispers. I heard them having sex. I could not sleep. Minutes passed by. The lizard moved to another part of the wall. I got up and crept on my hands and knees toward the lizard. Surprised that it had allowed me to get so close, I sat there and studied its leathery skin. Then I quickly grabbed it by the tail, but the lizard broke away and darted through the bamboo partition into the front room. Its tail wiggled in my hand. Frightened, I dropped the tail to the floor and watched it writhe. Moments later, its writhing stopped. I lay down on the mat again. An hour passed. I heard my mother and the soldier approaching the back room. Like always, I closed my eyes and pretended to be asleep.

"Wake up, you two," my mother said, and my brother and I opened our eyes. My mother gave us a mango in a brown paper bag, and the soldier handed us a six-pack of Coca-Cola. He smiled.

I jumped up, excited. Coca-Cola was an American drink. I popped the cap and relished the "whoosh" of the carbon as it escaped. While my brother and I drank the cold, sweet soda, my mother walked the soldier to the entrance of the alley. We followed them. On the street, the soldier got into an olive-green Jeep with white stars on its doors. He waved good-bye to us. My mother kissed him. Then he started the Jeep engine and all three of us watched its tires kicking up dust as he drove away.

"Is he my father?" I asked.

"Your father died," my mother said.

"Then, is he my father?" asked my brother.

"No. He's a friend."

"Will he take us to America?" I asked. My brother's eyes lit up with excitement. "Will he take us there someday?" he added.

"No," my mother responded and walked down the alley in silence. I studied my mother's face as she passed through shadow and sunlight. She was a beautiful woman.

In the back of the bungalow, I took the mango out of the paper bag. It was green, but it was a gift from the soldier.

"It isn't ripe," I told my mother.

"Put it in the rice jar," she said. "And wait for a week." I buried the mango in the rice of the clay jar. Every now and then, I put my hands over the clay lid and counted the days that had gone by.

"Don't lift the lid too soon, or the mango won't ripen," my mother warned. I wondered what the mango would look like, whether it would be orange or red. As the days passed, I swept dust from the corner where the jar sat like a shrine. I waited for the mango to ripen.

Recipe 3
Truong Tran

in the kitchen she kneads
white hot rice

with a damp cloth
forming pillow

a loaf of starch
her teeth anchor thread

to cut without clinging
tradition   necessity

nước mắm   chili peppers
a squeeze of lime

eating salty accommodates
this family of seven

Recipe 5

Truong Tran

the Vietnamese market on Sundays
sells hột vịt lộn
baby ducks   days from hatching

boiled   salted a delicacy
when eaten accurate   swift
straight from the shell

children are warned
ăn thì phải nhắm mắt lại—
when eating keep your eyes closed

The Bitterness
of Bodies We Bear

Bao-Long Chu

Tonight, my father combs my mother's hair down her back,
his hand gliding like a falcon over dark water. The years
since the war have bound them skin to skin, bone to bone.
She leans against him, or he against her, but beyond their bodies
embracing, merging, beyond this night, I see the certain, unbearable
grief of my mother's dying: a flaming coal in my father's mouth.

This vision, this impossible flower on fire I hold in my mouth
is nameless even as it names my life, names the hours and years
I see myself shadowed in a house, the shadow of my back
looming like a blackbird on the wall. Who can swallow this bone,
this shard of the future? This is the sorrow of bodies we must bear:
skin, tears, hair we shed. We eat the bitterness of bodies. Bodies

we love we embrace in brief repose, only to send off each body's
death with sighs, with prayers, with words, with our mouths
open, sweet with words. Even across sorghum fields and years,
even oceans and years, my father and mother will come back,
witnesses to this pain, relentless as the blood-flow between bones.
What I see is not my father standing behind my mother, her bare

back lovely, long against the length of his torso, but the unbearable
backside of Buddha turning away. What I see is my father's mouth,
a burning rose falling from it as he weeps over my sister's body
on Tu Do Street; what I see is the floating water, yellow backs
of monks heading up the hill where they will burn. I recall years
of waiting, waiting for a brother to come home. Finally his bones

came to us in a jar from across oceans. My mother took his bones,
white ashes between her hands, and breathed in the love of a body
she had endured. Believe me: this has everything to do with how I bear
my love for you—no, not my love of flesh to flesh, mouth to mouth
(though your mouth on my thigh and the curve of your back
are my nightly defeats). *These long mornings and years*

to come promise nothing, you say. But, love, the passing years
cannot undo; they deepen, shore the love, harden the lust we bear.
Come, let me take you in as my mother took in the love of a body
like a lover's grief for a body, her mouth taking in the powdered bones
of my brother; let me take you in as my father will soon, with his mouth,
take in my mother's death, his tongue holding onto, not pushing back,

the iron taste of death. Tonight, while you thrust your back
to me and against the coming years, I'll testify with my mouth
the truth of the body I bear: in you, I'll last beyond heart, blood, bone.

The Dill Peddler

Thanhha Lai

From her room Ba Nam can hear two scissortails calling her. She hushes them. She is almost ready, having twisted her silver hair into a bun and gotten dressed in black pants and a brown blouse and a gray sweater, all homemade, like the clothes her mother had worn, and so on, going back thousands of years.

Ba Nam steps off the back porch, flicks her hand at the birds and calls to them in a singsong tone that matches their own. "I know, I know, quit dancing in my ears. Do you want to wake my son?" The callers fly off. Duty done.

She strides around the yard, pausing at this plant and that plant, nodding. The dill is ready for market. The plants grow anywhere, by the swing set, in the sandbox, under the apple tree. Years ago Ba Nam had started an herb garden, but grass invaded every spot of exposed dirt. Only the dill grew, needing little care or water; wind would blow its seeds throughout the years, and every spring dill would sprout up, over the grass.

She squats by a cluster and begins snipping off branches, made up of millions of leaves tiny as ground pepper. It still amazes her that in a month new growths will replace the ones clipped. She places the branches in her basket, mindful of their delicate limbs; still, some crack and an overwhelming pungency invades the very back of her nostrils. She muffles her sneezes. "The young are fearful of outsiders, but the old must beware of those in their own home," she mumbles, and presses a hand to the damp earth to stand up. She walks with her back bent, as if to protect her basket, and moves to another cluster. Each time she squats down, her entire body pressing on weak legs, she grows more tired, yet the release of newly broken branches pushes her along. After filling her basket, she ties ten branches together to make a bunch. Fifty bunches in all.

"Tssk, tssk. Tssk, how can you turn to fire already?" she waves an index finger at the southern California sun. Still, her sweater stays on her, her way of appearing proper outside the house. Ba Nam is walking to the bus stop, her cane thumping the sidewalk with each step. She began those walks immediately after coming to this country; first she was unsure of her eagerness, then it occurred to her that here sewage is hidden and her steps land on gray, clean concrete. She is not sure what else she likes about this place, except its gray, clean concrete.

At times, she stops and unties her straw hat, running a wool-covered arm across her forehead. That hat, meant for American heads, had slipped off constantly, so she made straps for it from yellow and red cloth, bright as a ripe mango.

The same oily-skinned driver stops her. She tells herself not to look at him, but she does every time. Upon greeting her, his eyebrows bounce like writhing black caterpillars. She closes her eyes too late. He has always been here, from the first time her granddaughter took her on this bus, and he always wears what she wears, black pants and a shirt and a button-down sweater. He has the look of a Chinese peasant in the big city; she knows she does too and does not care. She hurries to the first row. Twice she had fallen when the bus pulled forward. He would be most attentive then, helping her to her seat and saying words that sounded strangely like *xin loi*, sorry in her language.

Near her stop she waves a tattered piece of paper at him. He knows without reading and lets her off at her stop.

Ba Nam hides in the crowds in front of Binh Dan Supermarket. It is a typical Saturday. Well-dressed young couples rush in and out, pushing and pulling groceries and children into their pace of life. She approaches them while they load the bags and holds their arms. Few get away.

She knows she is not supposed to sell there. In the past, the owner had paid her fifty cents per bunch, but some months ago she arrived late and lost her bid to another woman. The owner laughed when she refused his offer of ten cents a bunch. She then sold the dill herself, in front of his store. The first customer that day paid a dollar for a bunch, without bothering to bargain.

Last month the owner caught her and screamed that she was cheating him of profits. "You're the one robbing the guts from your customers' purses," she told him, swallowing her voice. She then sold her dill down the street, but it took all day to get rid of twenty-six bunches. "Why more people shop at the store of a man whose nose stands out like a snout on a tea pot, I'll never know," she mumbles. "French blood must have been in his family for a hundred years."

Ba Nam looks again at the sun and returns its stare. Tired of scolding it, and having sold twelve bunches, she looks for a place to sit. She thinks the broken chair too noticeable and settles for the support of a wall. She fumbles for her bag for *trau cau*. In foil, she had wrapped betel palm leaves and wedges of betel nuts and, in plastic, white limestone. She smears limestone onto the center of a leaf, then covers it over a wedge. The leaf is folded until it becomes skin around the wedge. She begins to chew and the bitter hotness stings her tongue, revives her. Eyes closed, she chews and turns toward the sun. A bit of juice, now turning red, slips down her throat; she lingers some minutes over the sensation of having peppers in her mouth, then spits the chew into a lidded Tupperware. Her son had warned that the juice will devour her intestines. She thinks him foolish. Did her villagers not live until a golden age? Besides, the chew leaves her breath fragrant and her teeth clean and strong.

Of her features, she is most proud of her shiny, black-lacquered teeth. During her courting years she was known for her teeth, and she is certain her husband chose her because of them. After all, her teeth testify to her discipline; some girls could not fast as well as she did, thus rubbing the medicine off their teeth, leaving them forever reddish brown. She lost more than ten kilos the month it took to dye her teeth. She is not sure how it was done, only remembering that she had to hold her mouth open for hours at a time while the herbalist applied endless ointments. First her teeth turned red, and she only ate rice soup that was poured down her throat. Eventually the medicine turned black and hardened around her teeth, protecting them from mouth worms.

Ba Nam sees a young woman who looks like a spender. She walks toward her, slower and more bent over than usual.

"Come here, come here. I have just the herb to make your sour catfish soup smell as pleasing as jasmine. Picked it this morning. It will hide the stink of any fish."

The young woman looks confused, accepts the bunch shoved at her.

"Just one dollar? It costs more than that for me to water it. Help me, please, what does it hurt?"

The woman laughs and gives another dollar. Ba Nam nods and smiles, thinking, "Young people, they throw their money away, but better to help an old woman than to spend it on their hair, making it stand like a porcupine's."

By early afternoon, she has sold thirty-four bunches. Ba Nam rubber bands the bills together and stuffs them in a pocket stitched to her underpants. She is careful to refasten the safety pin over the top of the pocket. During all the years when she sold vegetables in market, she kept her money this way and was never pickpocketed. She shivers thinking back to those days, when at five every morning she had to go bargain for vegetables from those who cycled them into the city from the fields, then she would sit in the market until evening reselling her goods to housewives. No one bought without bargaining; they haggled over the equivalent of a cent. That was how women of her class proved themselves.

She never questioned it then, the idea of marrying young and having babies and spending the majority of her life supporting them. Her husband brought home money during the good years, but when the war escalated he became yet another soldier. And died. It became her responsibility, all hers. She was proud, she remembers, proud of how she fed and clothed her family. Every widow did what she did, worked blindly for a common cause, not really knowing what it would bring, but she knew to do it. And now, her children grown, she wonders if she could have done something else, although that something else is as intangible as her reasons for doing what she did.

Someone drops something; when Ba Nam looks up, she thinks she sees the owner coming outside. She hurries toward the clothing store, head bent and body leaning hard against the cane.

She bumps into someone and would have fallen backward if two arms had not grabbed her. Her bag drops and bunches of dill spill onto clean concrete. A hand offers her a bunch. She looks up into the stern, oval face of a woman in a blue hat. "The snout nose must have called her," Ba Nam thinks.

As the woman mouths words, her fat cheeks jiggle. Ba Nam wants to laugh, but knows to act helpless.

"X-cu-xa-me I wan tu cole my sun," she enunciates her practiced line and hands over a note, written years ago, when she first insisted on riding the bus: "This is my mother. She does not speak English. If she shows you this note, it means she is lost and needs you to help her. Call me at 714-894-4420. I am her son, Mac Nguyen. Thank you."

Instead of a phone booth, the woman leads Ba Nam to her car. Ba Nam knows where they are going, and tells herself not to panic. Before she drives, the woman takes off her hat, showing that her hair is thick and black and is coiled on top of her head the way ancient Japanese women wore theirs.

Ba Nam glances at the woman's hair, turning away every time the woman faces her. She cannot tell if it is real, or if the woman has twisted fake hair into her own. Ba Nam knows of the possible harm, when lice and eggs could spread from the fake to the real and leave all worthless. She has seen it. The woman starts to talk and does not stop, reaching over and patting Ba Nam's hand. Ba Nam pulls her bag closer.

The sun, now hot as cooking oil, burns into Ba Nam's face. She wants to roll down the window, but the air conditioner is on. Artificial air hurts her lungs, and her intestines still twist like laundry each time the wheels are turned. "At least I am sitting," she thinks and leans back, tries to wiggle toes wedged inside tennis shoes her granddaughter had thrown away.

Inside the building, Ba Nam sees many people in blue. She breathes deeply, trying not to panic. After planning and planning, she has decided to tell her she was lost, like that time on the bus when he had to drive three hours to get to her. The woman faces Ba Nam and flips her wrist in front of her mouth. Ba Nam nods holding out seventy-five cents, not wanting charity. She sees a machine at the corner of the room and walks towards it. The woman calls after her; Ba Nam does not look back.

A man is kicking the machine. He should know that it only works with money, she thinks. The man turns around and Ba Nam's heart leaps a little. For a second she thinks it is the supermarket owner, the same French snout nose, so pointy that she looks up to see slits instead of full round nostrils. She touches her nose and wipes off the sweat. The familiar plumpness pleases her; for some seconds she circles her fingers on top of her nostrils, and their inflated flares remind her of the huge holes on the ground after a day underground. She looks again at the man's slits, thinking how sharp and secretive his nose must be. The man motions where the coins should go; Ba Nam does not smile back. She clutches her bag. They are pointing at her piece of paper. Ba Nam tries to understand, but as usual all she hears is the SSSSS and ZZZZZ of their snaky, hissy language. Once the man says, "Vietnam" and that soothes her. He nods and says, "Hello," before leaving. Ba Nam does not reply; instead, she stares at his inflated stomach, seen on so many American men. She imagines them eating chunks of meat big as her thigh, stretching their intestines, so that ten, fifteen years later the result droops like mounds of pig fat over the tops of their pants.

The woman calls the number. As she talks her lips sharpen to the shape of a parrot's beak. Ba Nam suppresses a giggle before holding her fist between her ear and mouth, asking to talk. The woman hangs up without looking at her.

Her son comes in. In short, jerky strokes he stabs back his bangs, flopped over his glasses like wilted lilies. He came from bed, Ba Nam knows, otherwise his hair would be sculpted in Vaseline. He has grown thin from overtime and his face looks even more ashen above his red shirt. On his feet are the same leather sandals that Ba Nam has nagged him to throw away. Jesus sandals, her granddaughter said they are called; they remind Ba Nam of the shoes of the Vietcong.

He ignores her and addresses the woman. Ba Nam whispers, "Tell her I was lost." He still ignores her. Neither looks at her. Their mouths open and close. Hisses. Ba Nam stands up when she hears, "Binh Dan Supermarket." They do not notice. She tugs at her son's sleeve three times, repeating that she was lost. No response.

"The policewoman says you were lost?" He finally turns to her.

"Children and animals! Yes, of course I was lost."

He grabs her bag, and opens it despite her resistance. He pulls out the dills, cracking their branches and scenting the air. More hisses. Ba Nam takes the dills from his hand and lays them in her bag. She breathes deeply; her head grows heavy. She sits down. The woman turns to her and clicks her tongue three times in admonishment while shaking her head.

Her son translates; she is fined seventy-five dollars for peddling food without a license and will be jailed should she repeat the offense.

"You never listen to your mother! I sent you to school to be a lawyer and you're smart as an ox."

He says nothing and they follow the woman to a counter.

Her son talks all the way to the car and in the car; at stop lights, he strikes the steering wheel and rages louder. Ba Nam rolls down her window. Despite the heat, real air calms her. She flips down the sun-blocker. They pass dozens of Vietnamese shops, offices, restaurants. This is the place to grow old, her son had said, this is where she can live in Vietnam without being in Vietnam. Ba Nam leans one ear against the wind, hearing coconut-leaf fingers dancing against each other. Her other ear still hears her son. She looks along the road. Tu Do Cafe...Thanh's Alterations..."Mother, you are my burden"...Two Crab Restaurant..."if we have to go to court"...Ba Le Sandwich Shop...Hien Khanh Dessert Shop..."clients can't know"...Banh Cuon Tay Ho..."be sweet like other mothers."

Near home, he calms down. His face deflates from puffy red to saggy gray, his eyes at once hostile and compassionate, as if he does not know what happened.

"Mother, please, you can't go outside and embarrass me anymore. Don't you want the Americans to think well of us? Do what you are capable inside the home. I'll give you money according to your needs."

She remains silent. For years she has been saving dollars given for tailor-made clothes and outings with friends. Why go to restaurants when food is cheaper and better prepared at home? Every weekend she and her friends used to meet. Now only two are left; the others have died or have followed their children to other cities. Back then, they saved money for an apartment, a place where they could all live together, eat what they want and play cards all night. The idea was so shocking it was funny. Then Ba Tu found out rent is six hundred a month for a dirty room in a place where the most recently-arrived live. Ba Nam continues to save, mostly for the clandestine thrill of ironing her bills late at night.

Then she got the idea to sell dill. By now, her shoebox is almost full of crispy bills. She hides the box in a different place every week, afraid her son will find it and force her to put it in his bank. Soon, she thinks she might join Ba Xuan on a trip to Las Vegas. From Ba Xuan's descriptions, it is all lights and cards. A bus would take them straight to a casino, with bedrooms upstairs, and all they would do is nap and play cards, nap and pull the machines for three lucky cherries, nap and ride the elevators to make their stomachs wiggle. There is even a chance to win back the cost of the trip; Ba Xuan has done it. Ba Nam has been thinking about it, but she loves the way the bills are filling her shoebox.

"Mother, are you listening? You have to sacrifice for your grandchildren's sake. You're embarrassing them. I know you like riding the bus, but I can't allow that anymore. We have to have order, have...."

"Sacrifice what? Isn't it enough I raised you and your brothers and sisters? No more. Sacrifice, ha. Sacrifice for what? I'm tired, I'm old, you sacrifice."

"Listen, mother, I know...."

"Enough. No more talk."

At home, her granddaughter runs out and asks too many questions. Ba Nam hands her the bag and goes to sit down. Her granddaughter stands at the sink and washes the remaining dill, her long hair rippling down her back. She suddenly yearns to see her granddaughter in shoulder-length hair and she thinks she might cut her own. For years she had said she would every week when she washed her hair.

"Father said I have to stay with you all the time."

"Foolish! Am I to go to school with you? Your father doesn't know what he means anymore."

"Are you in trouble?"

"Heaven and earth! I'm this old, what trouble could I be in?"

From the kitchen, she can see her son standing in the backyard, hands on his hips. The sun is behind him, still bright but starting to cool. These are her favorite hours, when she can anticipate the approaching coolness of dusk. Her son stares at the ground. Then he walks closer and closer to her dill plants, the ones near the swing set, and, bending down, casting his shadow over them, tugs at a plant. He stands up and walks away.

Ba Nam fixes her stare, and minutes later sees a lawnmower being pushed into the edge of her vision. Her son appears. She asks her granddaughter for *trau cau*; chewing, she asks for her dill. Sixteen unsold bunches. She walks to the sink, spits, empties her Tupperware, and sits back down to take off her shoes. She massages her feet, rolls her neck, and puts her shoes back on. Hearing the lawn-mower, she picks up her hat, cane, and bag, and walks out the door, knowing that she could catch the 4:42 bus, which would get her back to the market by 5:30, in time to meet the evening rush.

Copyrights

Acknowledgments

There are a number of individuals who were instrumental in bringing this publication to life.

We are indebted to Curtis Chin for planting the seed from which *Watermark* grew and for affording us the opportunity to cultivate it; to Christian Langworthy for his invaluable guidance; to our editorial assistants, Michelle Yung and Julie Ho, for managing the acquisition of permissions and contributors' biographies, and for the numerous hours of proofreading and typesetting; and to Thien Do for capturing the spirit of these works in his art and design.

We are grateful to Nguyen Qui Duc for his encouragement and sharp eye; to Russell Leong, Dan Duffy, and Thuy Linh Tran for helping get the call for submissions out and for putting us on the right trails; to Eric Gamalinda for his guidance in the difficult, early stages of planning; to Elaine Kim, Huynh Sanh Thong, and Luis Francia for lifting our spirits on the long journey to fruition; and to artist Kim Tran for continued generosity with his time, advice, and efforts, and for the donation of his print *A House Outside Hanoi, Vietnam*.

Melissa Rachleff of The Brooklyn Museum, Linden Chubin of The Asia Society, Catherine Coy of Poets House, and Martha Cinader of WBAI are all owed our sincerest thanks for the gift of their time and effort in getting the contributors to *Watermark* heard. We are also deeply grateful to Paul Slovak and Jim Geraghty of Penguin USA for making the impossible possible.

Our thanks are due also to Ngo Thanh Nhan for the tedious task of cataloguing; to Lisa Ko and Zahera Saed for hours of creative investigation and proofreading; to Neela Banerjee and Mari Pagliughi for the last minute once-over; to current and former AAWW staff members, Miwa Yokoyama, Ray Hsia, Derek Nguyen, and Erna Hernandez, for their indispensable behind-the-scenes assistance; to Andrea Louie for carrying the torch on; and to Peter Ong for his ongoing support in all facets of production and promotion.

There are also those to whom the editors are individually indebted:

Barbara Tran to her parents for a lifetime of encouragement; to Tyler and Will for support from the start; and to Bob for inspiration at the end of every day and for the much needed reminders.

Monique T. D. Truong to Damijan for his sustaining faith and spoons.

Luu Truong Khoi to his parents for their love and patience.

About the Contributors

Quang Bao was born in Can Tho, South Vietnam and immigrated to America when he was six years old. He currently lives in Northampton, Massachusetts and has just completed his first novel.

Lan Cao is a professor of international law at Brooklyn Law School and lives in New York. Born in Saigon, she left Vietnam in 1975. She is a graduate of Mount Holyoke College and Yale Law School and is the co-author of *Everything You Need to Know about Asian Americans* (Plume, 1996), as well as numerous articles in her field. She is a black belt in tae kwon do.

Bao-Long Chu's poems have appeared in *The Asian Pacific American Journal* and *The Viet Nam Forum*. He is currently Program Director for Writers in the Schools, a non-profit organization that places writers and poets in schools and community settings in and around Houston.

Linh Dinh was born in Saigon in 1963 and came to the U.S. in 1975. He has published short stories, poems, and translations in *Sulfur, Threepenny Review, American Poetry Review, Kenyon Review, New Observations, Denver Quarterly, Manoa, xconnect*, and the Vietnamese-language *Hop Luu, Tho*, and *Van Hoc*. In 1993, he was awarded a Pew Fellowship for poetry. Dinh has completed a compilation of Vietnamese folk poetry in translation, *The Cat Sits on a Palm Tree*, and he is also the editor and co-translator of the anthology *Night, Again: Contemporary Fiction From Vietnam* (Seven Stories Press, 1996). His short story collection, *Fake House*, will be published in the spring of 1999 by Seven Stories Press.

Maura Donohue was born in Saigon and raised in Rhode Island. She is the artistic director of In Mixed Company, and her work has been presented all over the East and West coasts. She choreographed lê thi diem thúy's *the bodies between us* for New Works for a New World and works regularly with Hung Nguyen and the LA-based Club O'Noodles. She's been commissioned by New World Theater to create a new work based on her recent return to Vietnam for their upcoming festival "VietNew: A Generation Emerges." She loves collaborating and invites Vietnamese artists to contact her at InMixedCo@aol.com.

Lan Duong is a graduate student at the University of California at Irvine in Comparative Literature, studying Vietnamese and French film and literature. She immigrated to San Jose at age two. She hopes to teach at the university level upon completion of her degree and eventually become an editor, working primarily with Asian and Asian American writers.

Huynh Sanh Thong is best known as a translator of Vietnamese verse (*The Tale of Kieu; The Heritage of Vietnamese Poetry; A Book of Vietnamese Poems*). For Yale he edited *The Vietnam Forum* and the *Lac Viet Series*. Now he edits *The Vietnam Review*, a semiannual collection of poems, stories, and essays. A MacArthur Fellowship, awarded in 1987, enabled him to complete a study of human origins. Here is his theory: "In the primeval jungle of Africa, threatened and obsessed, mothers mimicked snakes and thus learned to think, to speak, and to invent culture as a complex of serpent symbols."

Thanhha Lai lives in New York City, where she is enrolled in the graduate creative writing program at New York University. Her short stories have been published in *The Threepenny Review*, *The North American Review* and various anthologies.

Andrew Lam is an editor with the Pacific News Service in San Francisco and a regular commentator on National Public Radio. He was born in Saigon, Vietnam, and came to the U.S. at the end of the Vietnam War in 1975. His essays have appeared in *The New York Times, The S.F. Chronicle, The Chicago Tribune, The Baltimore Sun, The L.A. Times Magazine, Mother Jones, The Nation,* and other publications. His awards include the Society of Professional Journalists' Outstanding Young Journalist Award, The Media Alliance Meritorious Awards, The World Affairs Council's International Journalism Award, and the Asian American Journalists Association's National Award. Lam is currently working on his first short story collection.

Christian Langworthy is the author of *The Geography of War* (Cooper House Publishing Inc., 1995). Other poems appeared in *Premonitions* and *Muae* (Kaya Production, 1995), *Mudfish, Soho Arts Magazine, The Asian Pacific American Journal, Poet Magazine*, and an excerpt from his memoir was commissioned by WGBH of Boston for *The American Experience*. He has poems forthcoming in the anthology *From Both Sides Now* (Scribner, 1998).

lê thi diem thúy was born in South Vietnam and raised in Southern California. Some of her works appear in *The Very Inside: An Anthology of Writings by Asian and Pacific Islander Lesbian and Bisexual Women* (Sister Vision Press, 1994), as well as *The Arc of Love: An Anthology of Lesbian Love Poems* (Simon & Schuster, 1995). Her story, "The Gangster We Are All Looking For" first appeared in the *Massachusetts Review*, was reprinted in *Harper's*, and is included in *Best American Essays 1997* (Houghton Mifflin Company, 1997). She is currently working on a memoir of the same name, and a novel, entitled *The Bodies Between Us*.

Mộng Lan is a writer and visual artist. Her poetry is included in the anthologies *Once Upon a Dream: The Vietnamese-American Experience* (Andrews and McMeel, 1995) and *Making More Waves: New Writing By Asian American Women* (Beacon Press, 1997), as well as literary journals.

Bich Minh Nguyen was born in Saigon in 1974. Along with her family, she left Vietnam in April, 1975. She is currently working towards her M.F.A. in poetry at the University of Michigan in Ann Arbor, where she was awarded the 1997 Hopwood Award for Poetry for a manuscript that includes "Auspicious."

Nguyen Qui Duc is the author of *Where the Ashes Are* (Addison-Wesley Publishing, 1994) and the co-editor of *Vietnam: A Traveler's Literary Companion* (Whereabouts Press, 1996).

Minh Duc Nguyen is a graduate film student at the University of Southern California. He is now working on several screenplays.

Nguyen Ba Trac came to the United States in 1974 to pursue postgraduate studies in public administration. He is the author of two volumes of poetry, essays, travel writings, and short stories: *A Floating Blade of Grass* and *Tales of a Refugee with Average Headaches*. He is also the translator of an oral history of the fall of Vietnam compiled by Larry Engelmann, *Tears Before the Rain* (Oxford UP, 1990). Nguyen Ba Trac has been widely published in various Vietnamese literary journals and is currently a newswriter for several California newspapers serving the Vietnamese community.

Dao Strom was born in Saigon, Vietnam, in 1973. She grew up in Placerville, CA. She is a graduate of the University of Iowa Writers' Workshop, and her publications include *The Viet Nam Forum* and *The Southern Anthology*. She is the winner of the 1995 Nelson Algren Award.

Diep Khac Tran is a Vietnamese dyke living in Koreatown. She is a member of the Snazzy Writers' Workshop and the Women's Poetry Project in Los Angeles. So spoiled by both these groups, she's come to the conclusion that she can no longer write without participating in a workshop. Her work has appeared in *Dis-Orient* and *Doi Dien*.

Truong Tran is a graduate of the M.F.A. Program in Creative Writing from San Francisco State University, where he was selected as the 1995 Graduate Hood Recipient. He is also the recipient of the Browning Society Prize for The Dramatic Monologue, the Ina Coolbrith Prize for Poetry and the Arts Council of Santa Clara Fellowship in Poetry. His poems have been published in such journals as *The American Voice, Prairie Schooner, Crazyhorse, North Dakota Quarterly, Poetry East, ACM (Another Chicago Magazine), ONTHEBUS, Berkeley Poetry Review, Bakunin* and *ZYZZYVA*, among many others.

Trinh T. Minh-ha is a writer, filmmaker, and composer. Her more recent works include the books: *Drawn From African Dwellings*, in collaboration with Jean Paul Bourdier, (Indiana University Press, 1996), *Framer Framed* (Routledge, 1992), *When the Moon Waxes Red: Representation, Gender, and Cultural*

Politics (Routledge, 1991), *Woman, Native, Other: Writing Postcoloniality &* *Feminism* (Indiana University Press, 1989), *En minuscules* (book of poems, 1987); and the films: *A Tale of Love* (1995), *Shoot for the Contents* (1991), *Surname Viet Given Name Nam* (1989), *Naked Spaces* (1985), and *Reassemblage* (1982). She has taught at universities such as Cornell, San Francisco State, Smith, and Harvard, and is Professor of Women's Studies and Film at the University of California, Berkeley.

Trac Vu was born in Sai Gon in 1968. He left for Paris in 1980 and came to the U.S. in 1982. He received a B.A. in English from U.C. Berkeley in 1991. His writings have appeared in many publications, including the anthology *Best American Erotica 1995* (Simon & Schuster, 1995). He is currently in the M.F.A. program at U.S.C. School of Cinema-Television. His short *First Year* screened at the 1997 Sundance Film Festival, and he is working on a feature-length screenplay.

Thuong Vuong-Riddick was born in Hanoi. She studied in Paris. She taught French in both Saigon and Paris. In 1969, she emigrated to Canada and taught French literature at the University of Montreal, McGill University, and the University of Victoria. She published *Two Shores/Deux Rives* (Ronsdale Press, 1995) and lives in Delta with her husband and three children.

About the Editors

Luu Truong Khoi was born in Saigon and currently lives in New York City. His stories and essays have appeared in *Not A War: American-Vietnamese Fiction, Poetry, and Essays* (Yale University Council on Southeast Asia Studies, 1997) and *Once Upon a Dream: The Vietnamese-American Experience* (Andrews and Mcmeel, 1995). He received his A.B. from Harvard and his M.A. in Creative Writing from Boston University.

Barbara Tran earned her M.F.A. in poetry at Columbia University. Her works have appeared in *Amerasia, Antioch Review, The Asian Pacific American Journal, Pequod, Ploughshares, Seneca Review, The Viet Nam Forum,* and *Premonitions: The Kaya Anthology of New Asian North American Poetry* (Kaya Production, 1995), amongst other places. Tran has been in residence at the Millay and MacDowell Colonies.

Monique T.D. Truong is a writer and attorney living in New York City. Her short fiction and essays have appeared in *An Interethnic Companion to Asian American Literature* (University of Cambridge Press, 1997); *Asian American Literature: A Brief Introduction and Anthology* (HarperCollins College Publishers, 1996); *The Asian American Experience CD-ROM* (Primary Source Media and UCLA Asian American Studies Center, 1996), and journals such as *Amerasia* and *The Vietnam Forum.* Truong received her B.A. in Literature from Yale University and her J.D. from Columbia University School of Law.

A Note to the Reader

We have a memory of water. Ankle deep, back bent by the sun, verdant fields. Shallow basins, eyes sealed with tears, ornate cathedrals. Salt water shrouds, lips cracked, silent flotilla. We have a memory of water. A memory that is only sometimes our own.

As editors, we began the day with a plot of land and a selection of raw materials. We were asked to build a structure with only one constraint: it must hold water. We agreed on this one term, but agreed also that we should stick close to the landscape. The structure must hold water, yes, but we would make no attempts to redirect the flow or dictate its uses.

At the start of our work day, we found ourselves jaded and even a bit arrogant, our dark sides almost eager to fork human frailties and hidden weaknesses into the proper streams. By midday, however, we were no longer able to make simple judgments. We were scratching our heads, consulting our maps, calling our colleagues.

With *Watermark* now in your hands, we stop for a drink of cool water. We shield our eyes from the sun. We survey the landscape around us, search for those with dirt under their fingernails. We hope you are looking at your own hands in a new way.

The Editors

This publication is made possible
by generous donations from the following:

Anonymous (4)

Anne & Kirk Albers

Ben Allison/Sue Dimaggio

Nancy Bulalacao

Tam Thu Bui

Tonya Canada

Yasemin Celik

Gary L. Field

Henry Glosman

Dina Guttman

Dalila Hall

M. A. Jireret

Rani John

Gihwa Jung

Milly Lee

David LeMay

Barbara Li

Claire Li

Sophia Liang

Tyler Matney

Mike Muller

Dan-Thanh Nguyen

Hanh Nguyen

Minh Duc Nguyen

Nga Nguyen

Quan Nguyen

Peter Ong

Pharmaceutical Research Network, Inc.

Carol Remy

Laura Reuwee

Sylvia Reyes

Damijan Saccio

Joanne Saccio

Joseph Saccio, M.D.

Susan Cabranes-Saccio

Yasuhiro Saito/Barbara Rearick

Vera M. Scanlon

Holly Sheffer

Evette Soto

Jorshinelle Sonza

Eric Taitano

John Tan

Kim Tran

Son and Judy Tran

Thu Tran

Christina Truong

Lydia Tugendrajch

Kyoko Uchida

Ajoy Vachher

Angelo Verga/Mindy Gershon

James Verga

Jackie Vo

Leti Volpp

Joan L. Washington

Karen Kithan Yau

Kayoko Yokoyama

Zhou Xiaojing

This publication was made possible through the generous support of the New York State Council on the Arts, Jerome Foundation, and the City of Los Angeles Cultural Grant Program.

The Asian American Writers' Workshop is a not-for-profit literary organization devoted to the creation, development, and dissemination of Asian American literature, and is supported by the National Endowment for the Arts, the New York State Council on the Arts, the Department of Cultural Affairs, New York Community Trust, Jerome Foundation, Lannan Foundation, Greenwall Foundation, Witter Bynner Foundation for Poetry, Axe-Houghton Foundation, AT&T, Anheuser-Busch, Bell Atlantic, and Two St. Mark's Corporation, as well as by the generosity of its individual members.